The Footsteps
of a Prophet

By
Dr. Ed Dufresne

Ed Dufresne Ministries
Murrieta, California

Unless otherwise indicated,
all scriptural quotations are taken from the
King James Version of the Bible.

The Footsteps of a Prophet

ISBN 0-940763-21-4
Copyright @ 1989 & 2005 by
Ed Dufresne Ministries
P.O. Box 1010
Murrieta, CA 92564
U.S.A.

Published by
Ed Dufresne Publications
P.O. Box 1010
Murrieta, CA 92564
U.S.A.

Table of Contents

Other Books by Dr. Ed Dufresne

Devil, Don't Touch My Stuff

There's A Healer In The House

Fresh Oil From Heaven

Praying God's Word

Golden Nuggets for Longevity

Faithfulness: The Road to Divine Promotion

Anointing and Mantles

Faith that Makes a Demand on the Anointing

The Footprints
of a Prophet

Chapter One
Characteristics of a True Prophet

There is so much misunderstanding about the prophet's ministry, or office, that I want to examine it in this book. Also, the Lord has released me to do more teaching on the prophet's ministry.

With right teaching about this office, the Body of Christ will not be ignorant concerning the prophet's ministry, and those who are called to the office of a prophet will be helped to flow in their ministry.

The prophets must be before God and listen to what the Spirit of God is saying in this hour. The prophets must speak by the inspiration of the Holy Ghost!

The Lord spoke to my heart, "Revival won't come to America until the prophets get up and speak and prophesy." Teaching alone isn't going to get it. Pastoring alone isn't going to get it. Holding evangelistic meetings alone aren't going to get it. Unless the prophets speak what God tells them to say, our country is in trouble.

America needs prophets who can't be bought with a price - prophets who won't pimp their ministries for a price. We need prophets who will obey God.

We need the prophet's ministry to emerge to the forefront. We need to hear what the Spirit of God is saying through true prophets, and we need the prophets in this land to speak so we can have revival!

How many churches really teach on the prophet's ministry? Most Pentecostal denominations don't know much about

1

the prophet's ministry, and neither do many Full Gospel churches.

Someone told me that the pastor of a Full Gospel church said, "Well, God doesn't use prophets today. The prophet's ministry has been done away with." This was a Full Gospel minister who said that! When ministers don't understand the prophet's ministry, no wonder many believers in the Body of Christ don't understand it either.

On the other hand, another problem today is that many are going around saying, "I'm a prophet." Watch out for anyone who goes around announcing, "I'm this and I'm that," all the time!

Proverbs 18:16 says that your gift will make room for you. If the prophet's anointing is on you, people will recognize it. You won't need to tell it to everyone; there will be characteristics of the prophet's anointing present in your ministry.

There are nine major characteristics of a true prophet of God. Let's look at them.

A Characteristic of Revelation

The first characteristic of a true prophet is that he is a man of revelation. Much of the time he preaches or teaches by revelation. A prophet prepares for a service by feeding and meditating on God's Word, and by waiting before the Lord; but when he gets up and preaches, there's revelation that comes out of his spirit. Many times he'll preach things he's never planned on saying.

Sometimes, I'll go to the pulpit thinking I'm going to preach on a certain subject, but as soon as I get up there, other things start coming out of my spirit and I end up going a whole different direction. That's called preaching by revelation. I end up preaching things that are revealed to me at that moment.

It's important for the prophet to speak and bring revelation to the Church, for when a true prophet preaches and prophesies, revelation comes. Then the teachers who are set in the Church can build on that by teaching believers the revelation brought forth through the prophet.

A Characteristic of Knowledge

Resident in the prophet is the counsel of God. He's concerned with the things that are important to God. He has the heart and the pulse of God. Therefore, he can distinguish between the true and the false. This is the second characteristic of a true prophet

Jeremiah 23:16-18 reads,

> *Thus saith the Lord of hosts, Hearken not unto the words of the prophets that prophesy unto you: they make you vain: they speak a vision of their own heart, and not out of the mouth of the Lord.*
>
> *They say still unto them that despise me, The Lord hath said, Ye shall have peace; and they say unto every one that walketh after the imagination of his own heart, No evil shall come upon you.*
>
> *For WHO HATH STOOD IN THE COUNSEL OF THE LORD, and hath perceived and heard his word? Who hath marked his word, and heard it?*

A true prophet will spend time in prayer, hear the voice of the Lord, get the counsel of God, and then go out and deliver it, whether it's popular or not!

A false prophet will put vanity in you by puffing you up all the time. You see, there's a difference between exhortation and encouragement from a true prophet, and puffing people up from a hireling prophet.

There are a lot of Holy Ghost "nightclubs" and "bless-me clubs" around, where people prophesy over each other saying, "Well, this one's a prophet and that one's a prophet."

They're not. Those false prophets are just full of hot air.

Watch out for the person who butters you up all the time, saying things like, "Oh, you're great!" Nobody is great but the Lord Jesus Christ!

What else is Jeremiah saying in the passage we just read? Verse 17 tells us that false prophets prophesy out of their imagination. They imagine things.

Verse 18, on the other hand, says that true prophets are habitually before God, hearing the counsel of God, so they speak out what they have heard from God.

People frequently ask me, "Have you got a word for me?"

"Yes, I've got a Word for you! Read your Bible!"

I can't prophesy over anyone anytime I want. No one can turn the gifts of the Spirit on any time he wants to. That's not how it works. The anointing must come on you to prophesy, and that happens as the Spirit wills, not as man wills.

A Characteristic of Friendship

Amos 3:7 and Exodus 33:11 states that prophets are friends of God. That's the third characteristic of a true prophet.

> *Surely the Lord God will do nothing, but he revealeth his secret unto his servants the prophets.*
> Amos 3:7

> *And the Lord spake unto Moses face to face, as a man speaketh unto his friend…*
> Exodus 33:11

Another man who was a friend of God and who walked with Him was the prophet Enoch. *"And Enoch walked with God: and he was not; for God took him"* (Genesis 5:24).

Don't mess around with God's friends! As David pointed out, don't touch a prophet of God. *"Touch not mine anointed, and do my prophets no harm"* (Psalm 105:15).

David practiced this in his own life. Once, when King Saul was in hot pursuit of David and his men, David had a perfect opportunity to kill Saul in a dark cave, but his respect for the anointing of the Lord that was on Saul restrained him. David said to Saul, *"Behold this day thine eyes have seen how that the Lord has delivered thee today into mine hand in the cave: and some bade me kill thee: but mine eye spared thee; and I said, I will not put forth mine hand against my lord; for he is the Lord's anointed "* (I Samuel 24:10).

A Characteristic of Demonstration

The fourth characteristic of a true prophet is that prophets are men of demonstration. To reveal what God has given them, they often act out or demonstrate their sermons. To the carnal or natural mind their actions seem odd. But when these things are done in obedience to the Spirit of God, it blesses people.

Often, God will have me do unusual things in a healing line. He may tell me to jerk on someone's injured arm, or violently twist someone's injured neck. When I do this at the Spirit's direction, they always receive their healing.

One time another prophet spoke to me in tongues, but I heard them in English, which is scriptural (Acts 2:6-11). During another service, the power of God hit me and I began spinning like a top. Some people may think, "Oh, that couldn't be of God." But you haven't seen anything yet! God can move in a whirlwind, which is in line with the Bible. We're going to see some unusual manifestations of God's Spirit!

You can't figure God out! You can't figure Him out in your head – just jump in when He starts moving!

How do we know if it's God? Well, whoever gets the glory after it's done will tell the story right there.

Someone has to teach about these things because they're going to happen in this move of God, and we need to cooperate with Him and respond to the different ways He moves.

You Can't Call Yourself

Some people get it in their head that they're a prophet, and they go around giving out weird prophesies. But you can't call yourself to the prophet's ministry.

Sometimes people think they're a prophet, yet they don't even have a pulpit ministry. A prophet is going to have a pulpit ministry. You can't just be a layman in the congregation and stand in the office of the prophet. A pastor has a pulpit ministry. A teacher has a pulpit ministry. An evangelist has a pulpit ministry. Someone who stands in the office of a prophet would have to have a pulpit ministry.

Stay In Your Place

People cannot call themselves into the prophet's office. You get on dangerous territory when you try to operate in an office you're not called or equipped to stand in.

If you're a layman, be faithful to stay in your place in the Body of Christ, and serve in your local church. If you're in a fivefold ministry, stay in your own office, and don't try to function in one you're not called to. It's dangerous to try to walk in any office you're not anointed for. Intruding into the wrong office can kill you.

Don't get taken up with having a name or a title for yourself. Just stay faithful to God and let Him promote you in due season.

Many who are pastoring are not called to be pastors; they are really businessmen or just good administrators, but that doesn't mean they're equipped to stand in an office. When these businessmen try to pastor, they may die prematurely because they are not discerning their part in the Body of Christ. They are not where they belong. They will lose their effectiveness.

A Characteristic of Confrontation

Fifth, by nature, prophets are confrontational. It seems like they're always going a different way from the rest of the crowd. Also, prophets confront people with their sins.

Nathan confronted King David regarding his affair with Bathsheba declaring, "Thou art the man." Elijah confronted the prophets of Baal, then killed them all. John the Baptist confronted King Herod telling him that he was living in sin with his wife.

It doesn't make you popular when you go against the grain. I know what I'm talking about because I've been in churches where I've had to confront the pastor's wife who thought she was a prophet, and was trying to run everything. If you didn't bow down to her, she'd try to get rid of you one way or another, just like Jezebel tried to get rid of Elijah. As a matter of fact, I've been asked to leave some churches because I didn't recognize the pastor's wife as a prophet. If these Jezebels don't get their way, they have little "fits".

I believe in women who have the anointing of the prophet on their lives, but I don't believe in any man or woman who appoints themselves as a prophet. God has to anoint you to stand in that office.

Confrontation With a Jezebel

One night, after holding a conference in a hotel, a woman came after me in the restaurant. She started out, "I just want you to know, brother, that we love you." (Watch out for puffy, vain words!) "We love you and everything, but..." (Watch out for those "buts"!) "You know, my husband got offended by the way you prayed for him tonight."

I replied, "What was he doing in the line, then?"

"Well, you could have been more gentle about the way you put your hands on his head." (That's a religious devil talking!)

7

I thought, "Why isn't her husband over here telling me about it? Why is *she* telling me these things?"

And the Lord said, "She's got a Jezebel spirit." She was trying to run the man of God, just like Jezebel tried to run Elijah.

She continued, "Well, he didn't really want to go up there in the first place." (It turned out he was a minister in a large denomination that didn't believe in the operation of the gifts of the Spirit.)

I said just as nicely as I could, "Well, ma'am, he should never have gotten in the line."

She was trying to dictate to God and me how God should minister to her husband!

When God tells you to speak, you must say what God says. You're God's man or God's woman. You're God's friend. You hear God's voice. You get counsel from God.

Confrontation With Adultery

I was in a meeting once in the Midwest and all of a sudden God said, "This church is full of adultery. They're swapping wives."

I stood in front of the center section of that sanctuary and I asked two minister friends of mine who were present to stand in front of the side sections. I had everyone to pray.

I called for those men who were swapping wives to come up and repent. As you can guess, they didn't! So, I said to one of my minister friends, "Now, you go to that side section and God's going to lead you to one of the men. I'm going to go to this section over here." My other minister friend looked at me, and I've never seem him pray so hard in my life! I told him to go to the other side section and to pull out the man God led him to. He headed toward a man near the wall. God took him straight to the guilty man!

You talk about a confrontation and a demonstration by three men of God.

It didn't make me popular with the pastor. In fact, he never invited me back. The Lord was trying to help his church. The operation of the prophet's ministry brought light.

Shhh! Don't Talk Too Much

Before I start a meeting in a church, I don't want the pastor to unload all his church problems on me. Pastors sometimes start doing that when they pick me up at the airport, saying, "Well, we've got this problem and we've go that problem."

I'll say, "Shhh! Don't tell me anything, or I won't be able to help you." I need to minister to the whole church by the Spirit, and not by hearing all the problems of the church.

God will enable me to help pastors and their churches by the Spirit, but pastors must discern these gifts that God set in the Church. Pastors, that's why it's good to have the different gift ministries come into your church.

Private Confrontations

God has said to me, "Yes, I speak through prophets. The prophets are going to be saying some things to kings and heads of countries by the Spirit." Look at Proverbs 21:1. *"The king's heart is in the hand of the Lord...he turneth it whithersoever he will."*

Why will this happen? As we read in Amos 3:7, *"Surely the Lord God will do nothing, but he revealeth his secret unto his servants the prophets."*

God will reveal secret things to His prophets, and the prophets will have to obey what God said. However, this does not mean they have to do it publicly. Many people think a prophet must get up in front of a crowd in order to prophesy, but he can prophesy in his prayer time, or in a private gathering, and change things, dealing with things in the spirit realm as that anointing or mantle comes upon him.

A prime example of a man with the rank of "general" in the prophet's ministry was Kenneth E. Hagin. Although Brother Hagin was a teacher of the Word of God, he also stood in the office of the prophet. He was one of the prophets that God was using in these last days, before he went home to be with the Lord.

I use him as a prime example of the prophet's ministry because he's been my teacher. I sat under his ministry for over 30 years. He's the main prophet who made impartations into my life. He was in the ministry for more than sixty years, and his track record proves that he's been right on. He's a good example to follow.

Brother Hagin used to say jokingly that if he'd had his way, he'd go sit by a creek and eat wild onions. He wanted to live unknown and live a simple life. But the Spirit of God anointed his lips, and there were things he had to command in the spirit realm.

A Characteristic of Grief

The sixth characteristic of a true prophet is that prophets are saddened by what grieves God. They have the heart and pulse of God, so what grieves God grieves them.

I didn't understand that for years. Early in my ministry, when I would become grieved, I would think that the depression my mother had suffered from was coming on me. (I didn't know how to discern between spiritual grief and natural depression.)

Sometimes I'd be in a meeting, ready to prophesy, and all of a sudden I'd become grieved. Maybe the music would be totally wrong because the musicians were not in tune with God.

Once, I was considering holding a meeting in a certain church, but God said, "Don't do the meeting."

I found out they had dancers in their services – you know, women on tippy toes prancing around. Although there is a place for drama in the church, we're getting into things that sadden and grieve God.

Music, dance, or anything else that calls attention to the person, not to God, grieves Him – and I don't care how good the performance is! When I've been in churches that have dancers, I've sat on the platform and watched the men when those women dance, and those men weren't worshipping God! Why? Because the dancers wear skimpy little dresses and you can see everything. (Come to think of it, I've never seen a 500 pound woman dancing in those churches. They always get the skinny ones up there.) That's dancing in the flesh, and it grieves God.

Prophets are different. You can go all the way through the Bible and see that prophets are a different breed of person. Often they act saddened. "Grieved" is a better word.

I often get grieved. That means I've got to go apart and pray to find out what is grieving God. Then I've got to pray to see if it can be changed.

A Characteristic of Intercession

The seventh characteristic of a true prophet is that prophets are men of prayer.

Like Jesus, prophets often will go off by themselves to pray. That's why you must leave them alone sometimes. They need to get off by themselves.

Often, the spirit of prayer will hit me if I'm praying for someone. I was standing behind a fellow minister in a prayer line as he ministered one night. When his anointing would start to wane, the spirit of prayer would hit me, and I'd pray for him. The anointing would come on him stronger. Later, when I was ministering, he did the same thing for me. We need each other in the Body of Christ.

In prayer, the prophet not only speaks to God about men, but he speaks to men about God. For example, in Exodus 32:7-42 Moses prayed for the children of Israel.

The prophet Samuel was inconsolable at King Saul's downfall. *"Then came the word of the Lord unto Samuel, saying, It repenteth me that I have set up Saul to be king: for he is turned back from following me, and hath not performed my commandments. And it grieved Samuel; and he cried unto the Lord all night"* (1 Samuel 15:10, 11).

A Characteristic of Hope

The eighth characteristic of a true prophet is that he is a man of expectation, faith, and hope. We've all heard prophets of gloom and doom. All they speak is damnation and doom. Don't listen to them!

Some of them have prophesied that California is going to fall into the ocean, and the new beach is going to be in Arizona! Every time California has an earthquake, here come the doomsday prophets, shaking their heads and saying, "Yeah, 'the big one's' coming!"

California isn't going anywhere. There are a lot of covenant people there.

You also have to watch out for the prophet who prophesies in vain to you. They're the ones who try to get you to walk in vanity. They say, "Thus said the Lord, you're going to be a great man of God." Remember, without God, you're nothing. I was nothing when God got hold of me, but in Him I am the righteousness of God.

A true prophet of God may give you a warning from God, but he also will give you light – the revelation or answer for how you can change the thing God is showing you.

The true prophet is also a man of restoration, like Daniel and Moses. He brings men back to God, and he brings God back to men. That's one reason why prophets are so important to the Body of Christ today.

There will always be faith and hope in messages delivered by true prophets, because they produce faith and hope. The Bible says if you listen to the prophets, you'll prosper. "...*Believe in the Lord your God, so shall ye be established; believe his prophets, so shall ye prosper*" (2 Chronicles 20:20). Notice it says, "Believe his prophets." Believe them! You will prosper by listening to God's true prophets.

Several years ago, many prophets prophesied, "Be careful in the next two years. Don't get too far in debt." Those who didn't listen to them went ahead, got in debt, and many lost everything they had.

I got up to preach one Sunday morning in Los Angeles, and all of a sudden I prophesied that gold was going to double in value, and it did!

You'll remember that Brother Hagin said at his 1987 Camp meeting that if Christians didn't pray, and if the wrong man became President of the United States, the economy of this country would be in a big mess.

Some will argue, "Well, I don't care about the economy. God is going to take care of me." That's being selfish. It would be difficult for you and other Christians to preach the Gospel and live in peace if your bills weren't paid.

When the prophets of the land speak and changes are made by the Spirit of God, the rest of the Body will be blessed.

A Characteristic of Humility

The ninth characteristic of a true prophet is that he is a man of meekness and humility. He never conveys the impression that he's infallible.

One thing that grieves God is when we give men the glory. We can have men we honor, but we must be careful that we don't worship the leaders of spiritual movements. If we do, we'll start seeing their crowds dwindle, because God is the One who must get all the glory.

The true prophet always gives the impression that he is willing to have his life, his ministry, and the way he operates in the gifts be evaluated and judged by those of equal or higher anointing.

In First Corinthians 14:29, Paul writes about prophets judging things that are done in services, *"Let the prophets speak two or three, and let the other judge."*

Then he says in First Thessalonians, *"Quench not the Spirit. Despise not prophesyings. Prove all things; hold fast that which is good. Abstain from all appearance of evil"* (1 Thessalonians 5:19-22).

Chapter Two
"I Ordained Thee a Prophet"

It is imperative that you know beyond any doubt that you are called of God to be a prophet. Your call must be confirmed until absolutely no doubt remains in your mind because, as James says, *"A double minded man is unstable in all his ways"* (James 1:8).

If I were on an operating table and a qualified doctor came in, saying, "Well, I don't know if I can do this or not," I'd yell, "Get this guy out of here!" He'd better have confidence in what he's doing before he operates on *me!*

Regardless of the call on your life, it's essential that you have complete assurance about your ministry. Many of you went to Bible school to find out. You felt a call, or you had an urge to do something for God. It usually takes a while for that urge to progress to the point of total assurance.

You can know if you have a divine call by *conviction,* by a *witness* in your spirit, and by a divine *compulsion* on the inside of you concerning the call that's upon your life. You can even know if you're called to be a prophet or not. It's the same way you can tell if you're a pastor or not. The characteristics of that mantle will be on you!

Prophecy Confirms, Never Calls

If someone prophesies that you are called to the fivefold ministry, but God hasn't told you, disregard the prophecy!

Sometimes I'll go to a church and a young man will get me

in a corner, or slip into the pastor's office and whisper, "I'm a prophet."

I always reply, "Oh yeah? How do you know?"

He'll say, "Well, a guy here prophesied," or "Someone came through and prophesied over me that I'm a prophet. Uh, what do you do as a prophet?"

"Well, I work. I work in the Gospel. I don't sit up on a mountaintop and prophesy all the time."

The true New Testament gift of prophecy only confirms, it never calls. Years ago, when people started prophesying over me about the different callings on my life, I already kind of knew about them. The whole picture was still fuzzy to me, but their words confirmed what God was already dealing with me about.

Needs vs. Calls

A need is not a call. Some people see a need, so they try to call themselves into the ministry in order to fulfill that need. In other words, just because they are burdened for Mexican orphans doesn't mean they are called to be a missionary to Mexico. Sometimes it's just a burden to pray.

If you enter the ministry and God didn't call you, you will fail; but if you have that divine call and remain faithful to it, you will succeed.

I've known young men who have wanted to get involved in the ministry. They've said, "God told me to do this for you. God told me to do that for you." But after a while, when the going got tough, off they went. They weren't called.

The Fight for Your Ministry

The devil will fight you for that call of God that's on your life. He will try to talk you out of it. He doesn't want you in the position that God put you in.

There will be rough times in the ministry, but you must remain faithful to your call during those times. You see, there's a price you pay to walk in the anointing!

You may be called upon to make great sacrifices, but the call alone will pull you through if you remain faithful. That's one way you can tell if you've got the call. Just remain faithful to it, and that call will pull you through.

If you think you are called to stand in a particular office, wait and test your call to find out for sure. Even if you are called to one of the ministry offices, you won't step into it immediately; you'll start at the bottom.

If God exposed you to the full power of the office while you're still in training, it could destroy you and your ministry. You haven't learned how to be faithful yet. You haven't learned how to be consecrated yet.

Can you imagine a little baby playing in his crib with an H-Bomb? What if his daddy gave it to him and said, "Now, just push that button, and you'll have all the power you want." It's the same with the fivefold ministries. There's a lot of power in them, and it takes time – years, in fact – to learn how to operate them.

The Years of Preparation

When I was just starting out in the ministry, I was holding a morning teaching service, and the power of God fell. I told a young man what God was showing me about him. Later, I felt I had grieved the Spirit of God.

I asked, "What is it, Lord?"

He said, "You shouldn't have told him. I revealed it to you, but you weren't to tell it now. You could have hurt him because he's so enthusiastic. But he'll be all right. You pray for him."

That's how I learned that there's a time to reveal things by the Spirit, and there's a time not to say those things.

Brother Hagin was in the ministry for eighteen years before he entered into the prophet's ministry, but that prophet's anointing didn't come on him until he had been in the ministry for eighteen years!

If you are called to the fivefold ministry, use your years of preparation to study. Preparation time is never lost time.

Whatever your call is, you must build your ministry on the Word of God. You cannot build a ministry on the supernatural, or on a gift. If you will build your ministry on the Word of God, it will last, because the Word is forever.

Dedicate, consecrate, and submit yourself to God's will in your life. Know that if God calls you, He will equip you to carry out that call. Your gift will make a way for you. Also, as you are preparing for your call, get involved in a local church. Do whatever your hands find to do in the ministry of helps.

Dusting the Pulpit

I served in the ministry of helps for years, and I'll never forget the night I was dusting the pulpit, and all of a sudden a voice boomed out of the pulpit, saying, "You'll go all over the world and preach." I jumped! I looked and no one was around.

I thought my pastor was playing a practical joke on me, so I walked over to the loudspeaker and inspected them. But it was God speaking to me.

I replied, "God, I can't even get up and give a testimony, much less preach! That ain't my calling. I'm a helper. I work with my hands. I can build buildings, and I can clean toilets, but I can't preach."

Even my pastor told me, "Ed, you'd have to go to speech classes for ten years before you could preach." If I'd have listened to him, I wouldn't be in the ministry today. But here

I am, mistakes and all. I was faithful where I was, and a faithful man shall abound in the blessings of God!

As you remain faithful wherever you're at, God will bring you to the top. It happens every time. Cream always rises!

Called From My Mother's Womb

Yes, there are times when my knees shake when I get up to preach. However, I know what God has called me to do.

The Bible tells us in Isaiah and Jeremiah that a prophet is called from him mother's womb. One day the Lord gave me a vision of my whole life and revealed to me that I was called from the womb. He explained my whole life up to that point in time.

For years, I didn't realize that the prophet's mantle was on me. This knowledge gradually unfolded to me. Things started happening and God dealt with me about the anointing on my life. However, I didn't understand much about it because there was a lack of teaching on the office of the prophet in those days.

Different men of God would come to town, call me out of the congregation, and prophesy about my ministry, but I was still in the ministry of helps then. I had the ministry of toilets.

That's right! For five years I cleaned the church toilets. Not too many ministers want to start out by cleaning toilets, but God's got to find out if you're faithful. If you can't clean toilets for God, how are you going to prophesy for Him?

When the Lord started dealing with me about ministry, I reminded Him, "Lord, I'm not an eloquent speaker." I could never get up and give a talk in grammar school, junior high, or high school (which I didn't finish). There were too many problems at home. My home was full of alcoholism, and I couldn't study under those circumstances, so I dropped out of school.

Several years ago, when the Lord gave me that vision of my life, He said, "Ed Dufresne, I know you. I ordained you and I sanctified you in your mother's womb to be a minister of the Gospel."

Angels Halted My Abortion

In the vision, He showed me that my parents had decided to abort me a few weeks after I had been conceived! That was in 1940. My mother was 15 years old and my dad was just 16. Also, World War II was about to break out.

My dad was an apprentice sheet metal man, and he couldn't afford to get married. So they talked about aborting me, and my mother was ready to go for the abortion.

In the vision, I saw what happened. I saw angels come down from heaven and stop it, because God commanded that I was ordained of God. The angels turned the situation around and my parents got married instead of having the abortion.

I was born in June, 1941. I'm here. But if they had aborted me, I'd still be a human being, and I'd be in heaven now.

Let's take a little side trip here. When you get to heaven, you're going to see all the aborted children. They're there. Once when God was dealing with me about an unwed mothers home, I had a vision and saw these aborted children in heaven. I also saw the women who had aborted their children. They thought they had gotten rid of them. (It's absolutely shocking to me that even Christian women get abortions. Some of them, of course, later repent, and they can be set free of their sin and guilt.) I saw, as the saved women walked through the gates of heaven, their little aborted children were saying, "Mommy, I love you!"

Until the Lord showed me this vision, I had never known that my parents had considered aborting me. Later, I asked my dad about it. He said, "Yes, sorry to say, that's true. We were going to abort you."

The Devil's Plot Against Prophets

The Lord revealed many other things to me. He went all the way through my life and showed me many past events, explaining why things had happened and why people had behaved the way they did.

I had many relatives on both sides of the family who were in mental institutions. When my grandfather found out my mother was pregnant with me, he committed suicide. He left a note to my mother, telling her that's the reason he committed suicide; he couldn't handle her pregnancy. Then, of course, my mother had to live with that guilt the rest of her life, and that's what drove her into mental institutions.

After my parents married, they vowed they weren't going to drink alcohol like their families did. But as time went on, they started sipping little cocktails and having a little wine, and they did end up as alcoholics.

All of these things were geared to destroy that anointing that came out of my mother's womb – her son who was ordained a prophet.

The devil hates anointed men and women of God. He hates Christians, and he seems to particularly want to destroy prophets!

Look at Brother Hagin's life. He was born prematurely. He didn't even look like a human baby. The doctor and his Grandmother Drake couldn't detect any signs of life, so his grandmother was going to bury him in the back yard! But his angels intervened to protect him, and his grandmother suddenly detected a little movement in the tiny body. He went on to fulfill the ministry God had for him, and he was in his 87th year when he went home to be with the Lord.

I appreciated God so much for taking me all the way back through my life and explaining everything that has happened to me. I learned that all the bad things were planned by the devil to destroy the anointing that has been on my life from my mother's womb.

The devil is working overtime to destroy the anointing on the lives of all of God's servants. That's why we shouldn't get angry at the person who has fallen to Satan's wiles. We have no right to criticize such a person. We don't know all the stress and strain he has been under. We should just keep quiet and pray for him.

God's Call to Isaiah and Jeremiah

The Lord gave much the same commission to the prophet Isaiah that He did to Jeremiah.

> *Listen, O isles, unto me; and hearken, ye people, from far; The Lord hath called me from the womb; from the bowels of my mother hath he made mention of my name.*
>
> *And he hath made my mouth like a sharp sword; in the shadow of his hand hath he hid me, and made me a polished shaft; in his quiver hath he hid me;*
>
> *And said unto me, Thou are my servant, O Israel, in whom I will be glorified.*
> Isaiah 49:1-3

The following passage from Jeremiah reveals how God looks at His prophets. This is the assurance He gave the prophet Jeremiah.

> *Before I formed thee in the belly I knew thee; and before thou camest forth out of the womb I sanctified thee, and I ordained thee a prophet unto the nations.*
>
> *Then said I, Ah, Lord God! behold, I cannot speak: for I am a child.*
>
> *But the Lord said unto me, Say not, I am a child: for thou shalt go to all that I shall send thee, and whatsoever I command thee though shalt speak.*

Be not afraid of their faces: for I am with thee to deliver thee, saith the Lord.

Then the Lord put forth his hand, and touched my mouth. And the Lord said unto me, Behold, I have put my words in thy mouth.

See, I have this day set thee over the nations and over the kingdoms, to root out, and to pull down, and to destroy, and to throw down, to build, and to plant.

(Jeremiah 1:5-10)

Let's begin with the fifth verse: *"Before I formed thee in the belly I knew thee; and before thou comest forth out of the womb I sanctified thee..."* Isn't it amazing that people will abort children? Their excuse is, "Well, that was nothing but a blob." But here God says, "I knew them before they were even formed. In the belly I knew them." You don't know a blob!

"And before thou comest forth out of the womb I sanctified thee..." This means that God set the prophet apart. *"...and I ordained thee a prophet unto the nations."* (Did you know there are different degrees of prophets? Some prophets are appointed over specific cities or nations.)

"And God Hath Set Some in the Church"

First of all, God is the One who calls someone to the ministry. God does this, not dad, mom, family, or church boards. You can't set yourself apart as a prophet or any other gift ministry. You've got to be commissioned or ordained by God.

I believe in the fivefold ministries that God sets in the Church.

AND GOD HATH SET SOME IN THE CHURCH, first apostles, secondarily prophets, thirdly teachers, after that miracles, then gifts of healings, helps, governments, diversities of tongues.
1 Corinthians 12:28

> *AND HE GAVE SOME, apostles; and some, prophets; and some, evangelists; and some, pastors and teachers; For the perfecting of the saints, for the work of the ministry, for the edifying of the body of Christ.*   Ephesians 4:11, 12

One day I was reading First Corinthians 12:28, and I asked the Lord, "What do You mean by 'set'?" My mind immediately went back to the years I was in construction work. I know what happens when concrete sets up.

When we poured concrete and it was still wet, we could move it around; but once it was set, we couldn't move it unless we dynamited it. God sets ministries in place.

It amazes me that people think they can call themselves into the ministry! I saw a TV preacher who said, "Bless God, if we need a prophet in our church, God will anoint me to be the prophet. If we need an apostle, He'll anoint me to be the apostle."

I thought, how ignorant can you get? That isn't what the Bible says. The Bible says, *"And God hath set some in the church..."*

Men can't set the fivefold ministries in the Body of Christ!

No Man-Appointed Offices

A healthy local church is one where the congregation is exposed to all of the fivefold offices. But, the leadership can't appoint the fivefold gifts into their local church. The fivefold offices are set in the entire body of Christ, but they don't have to be set into each local church. Yet, I see a very great error abroad right now in the Body of Christ. What is happening is that men with good intentions, who are trying to go along with what they think the Bible says, are electing someone who prophesies as their prophet – with disastrous results. They're also taking it upon themselves, in the flesh to set their own apostles in their churches; men they allow to run the church.

But the pastor is to run the church. He's the highest authority in the church. In fact, if the pastor pioneered that church, he's the apostle of that church.

I've been in churches where people pointed out certain men and said, "This is our apostle, and this is our resident prophet."

I don't know why, but many of the so-called prophets are big old guys. They sit on the platform looking gruff – for that's how they think a prophet should look – and they strut around, saying, "Thus saith the Lord…" No, thus saith them! They're not true prophets. I call them "hireling prophets."

Once, when someone said, "He's a resident prophet," God said to me, "No, he isn't. Men set him in there, because they're trying to set up their idea of a New Testament Church."

I've seen shipwreck in people's lives because of these so-called "resident prophets." The church leaders have told them, "You're our resident prophet – now prophesy!" So, they've prophesied, "Thus saith the Lord, give me your house." Or "Thus saith the Lord, you married the wrong person. You're to leave your husband."

That's nothing but a bunch of junk! But there are people who would rather hear the lies of false prophets than hear the truth. They want to hear what they want to hear.

But there are true prophets that are a great blessing to the Body of Christ, and we need to learn about that important office, and pray for them to operate in the full measure of that office.

The Prophet's Strength

Jeremiah protested, *"Ah, Lord God! Behold, I cannot speak: for I am a child. But the Lord said unto me, Say not, I am a child: for thou shalt go to all that I shall send thee, and whatsoever I command thee thou shalt speak"* (Jeremiah 1:6, & 7).

That's a strong word. There's something about a prophet

under the anointing of God. When he says something that God commands, it's stronger. It goes deeper into the spirit realm. It can change cities.

I didn't even know these verses were in the Bible when God first dealt with me concerning my call. He said to me, "You will obey, and you will command what I tell you."

"Be not afraid of their faces: for I am with thee to deliver thee, said the Lord" (verse 8).

Sometimes a prophet needs to be delivered from the fear of what people will say. This doesn't happen overnight, however. Several years ago it got me in trouble. God dealt with me about it. He told me, "You've been afraid of man, and sometimes you'll hesitate and back off because of criticism and what people say."

Whatever ministry you're in (or even if you're not in the ministry), you're not to be afraid of other people's opinions. In other words, don't let people talk you out of your healing, your prosperity, your calling, or anything else God gives you.

"Then the Lord put forth his hand, and touched my mouth. (I remember when God did that to me.) *And the Lord said unto me, Behold, I have put my words in thy mouth"* (verse 9). When God touches your mouth, your mouth is never the same!

Tear Down and Build

Jeremiah 1:10 illustrates why it is essential that pastors recognize the prophet's ministry and invite prophets to come to their church. *"See, I have this day set thee over the nations and over the kingdoms, to root out, and to pull down, and to destroy, and to throw down, to build, and to plant."*

As this verse points out, prophets root out, pull down, destroy, throw down, build, and plant. That means they root things out that need to be rooted out – evil spirits, religious teachings, and whatever else needs to be changed. The whole direction of a church can be corrected.

Notice what else prophets do. They build and plant! After they "clean house," they leave a church in better condition than when they came. That's one reason why God set this mantle in the Body of Christ.

A prime example of this took place in a meeting in Tulsa. Brother Hagin said by the Spirit that there was a pastor present who was so discouraged by the behavior of certain men on his board that he was about to resign.

By the Spirit, Brother Hagin gave the first names of these trouble-makers; then he advised the pastor not to quit, because God was going to turn the situation around.

That brought light. It brought revelation and straightened things out. It wasn't negative. The Spirit of God nailed the devil and a bunch of deacons! Glory to God!

It was done publicly, but as we saw earlier, a prophet does not necessarily have to prophesy publicly in order to be effective. A prophet can do that in his prayer time, or in his own bedroom. When that prophetic anointing comes on him, things will be said by the Spirit of God that can change cities, nations, kingdoms, and other aspects of the spirit realm.

Spiritual rankings are similar to military rankings. God's generals deal with Satan's generals, lieutenants deal with lieutenants, corporals deal with corporals, captains deal with captains, and so on. That's another reason why we need the prophet's ministry. They will be able to deal with things that other offices aren't anointed to deal with. If you teach them right, your congregation will know how to "pull" on the prophet's gift. They'll know what to do and what not to do when his gift goes into operation.

If pastors would discern the prophet's ministry and have prophets visit their churches, there wouldn't be as many messes in the church.

A pastor told me his church was going down the tubes. He invited me to minister there. Afterwards, he wrote me, saying, "I don't know what happened, but as a result of some of the things you said, our finances have changed. There's also a stronger healing anointing in the church."

What happened? The Lord revealed some things by the Spirit of God that needed to be rooted out. There were some things in the spirit realm that had to be dealt with through the prophet's anointing.

Yes, the Holy Spirit is our Teacher and our Guide and, yes, teaching is valid – don't misunderstand me – but the teacher's anointing wouldn't have been effective in that case. It required the prophet's anointing, which is a stronger and different anointing.

Prophets and Teachers

Prophets speak revelations that teachers can build on. There are certain things that still need to be said by the Spirit of God. As prophets deliver what Gods wants said, the teachers can then take what God said through the prophet and continue feeding that revelation to the people.

Several years ago I heard one speaker say, "We really don't need a revival in our churches today as much as we need the prophet's ministry to come forth. Now, we do need revival in our churches," he added, "but when the prophets come and speak, that will bring revival."

I believe we're going to start seeing this. Some of the prophets are going to start teaching on this. They're going to root out and pull down. Churches will change.

The pastors will notice the changes brought through the prophet's mantel. They'll say, "We don't understand it. You got up here under the anointing of God and spoke some things and – boom – things changed. The finances changed. Things changed spiritually."

That's the ministry of a prophet. Do you understand the importance of it? The devil does. He's been trying to hinder them, but now the true prophets are coming on the scene, and they're going to obey God.

The true prophets will say things by the Spirit that we'll use to build a foundation to ride on into this next wave.

We read where Jeremiah was told he would root out, pull down, destroy, and throw down. But he was also told that prophets build and plant. The Church will build and plant on the foundation established by the prophets.

Prophets Are Seers

In Jeremiah 1:11-13, the Lord asks the prophets, *"Jeremiah, what seest thou? And I said, I see a rod of an almond tree. Then said the Lord unto me, Thou hast well seen: for I will hasten my word to perform it. And the word of the Lord came unto me the second time, saying, What seest thou?..."*

Remember, the prophet is a seer, He sees things. We could say, as some do, "The prophet is the eye of the Body of Christ." What prophets see, they tell the Body of Christ. When a seer sees something and then speaks it, God will perform it. That's why the prophet's words won't fall to the ground.

For example, I've read how Brother Hagin was in the Spirit when ministering to cancer patients on several occasions. He was caught up by the Spirit into another realm, saw or discerned the evil spirit hanging onto its victim, and dealt with it. The demon left, and the person was delivered. When he dealt with the demon causing that cancer, all the people were healed.

Prophetic Warning

I would prefer to use someone else as an example, but this actually happened to me. One Sunday morning I was preaching in my first church in California, I was caught up in the Spirit and saw that someone was going to try to kill the President of the United States. I told the congregation,

"Pray, pray, pray!"

Soon after that, a young man tried to assassinate our President, but he didn't succeed.

Can you imagine what would happen if we did away with the prophet's ministry? What God revealed that morning brought light and illumination.

We read in Amos 3:7, *"Surely the Lord God will do nothing, but he revealeth his secret unto his servants the prophets."* Until the Lord reveals it to the prophets, He won't do anything. He will do nothing unless He reveals it to His prophets. That's what I mean about the light coming to the Body of Christ.

The Prophets: The Eye of God

We can see this stated as a paralled truth in Luke 11.

> *No man, when he hath lighted a candle, putteth it in a secret place, neither under a bushel, but on a candlestick, that they which come in may see the light.*
>
> *The light of the body is the eye: therefore when thine eye is single, thy whole body also is full of light; but when thine eye is evil, thy body also is full of darkness.*
>
> *Take heed therefore that the light which is in thee be not darkness.*
>
> Luke 11:33-35

The prophet is the eye, bringing light to the Body of Christ. When the prophet speaks, he brings light and revelation for the Body, giving direction. Then, as we saw earlier, the teachers will build on that foundation the prophet has laid.

Of course, we are not led by prophecy or by prophets. We are led by God's Spirit and His Word. On the other hand, the Bible says that if we believe His prophets, we shall prosper. Furthermore, we can be led into the light that a prophet brings by the Spirit of God.

Bear in mind that a prophet must be proven, mature, and walking obediently before the Lord with a pure heart. Also, a true prophet should prophesy in line with the Word of God. If what he says isn't in line with the Word of God, you don't want to listen to him.

I judge the things prophets and others say according to the Word of God. I also judge the fruit in the person's life. No, I'm not talking about the kind of clothes he wears or the kind of car he drives. I'm talking about his spiritual track record. Is he seasoned? Does he have the right kind of character? What about his love walk – does he walk in love?

If a prophet is rebellious, I don't want to hear him. If he's one of the little "hot airs" going around watching X-rated movies and living in the world, I'm not going to listen to him. He can't be a prophet and have a worldly spirit. That harlot, the world, will get your power if you play with it!

Darkness or Light?

True prophets are speaking today, but if the Body of Christ refuses to listen or obey, we're going to be in darkness and bondage. If the Church only realized that the prophet brings light to set you free, not put you in bondage.

True prophecy enhances and confirms the Word of God; it never violates or contradicts it. Also, true prophecy produces a new flow of life, not bondage.

How to Miss the Voice of God

We often close our ears to sensitive areas in our life, for the flesh wars against the things of the Spirit. So, God in His wisdom, has the prophet to speak what we don't want to hear. There are adjustments that we need to make, and the prophet helps us make them.

I wonder how many movements of God we've already missed because the Church would not listen, preferring to continue in their rebellion. That's why there are all kinds of dead denominational churches on every corner. They didn't listen to the prophets of the land and build on the new foundation they were trying to lay; years have gone by, and those dead churches remain unchanged or they lacked discernment and listened to the wrong prophet.

How to Miss the Call of God

If you are a dippy, half-dedicated Christian who is messing around with the things of this world, you won't be conscious of God speaking to your spirit, and you could very easily miss the call of God!

Furthermore, if you start playing with worldly things, like watching sports or movies all the time, and you don't spend time before God and get involved in church and with the things of God, you could miss the call of God!

Chapter Three

Different Ranks and Different Anointings

B efore a minister can press further into the spirit realm, they must first be equipped to do so.

Everyone thinks a minister should be able to do everything, but he can't. Ministers in the modern Church, however, are trying to be a jack-of-all-trades.

A minister can get off by getting into activities that God never called him to do; even spiritual activities. So, it's important to find out exactly what God has called you to do, and then do it. Remain in your place, or rank, in the Body of Christ.

Any ministry gift carries different ranks within that office. Romans 11:29 & 12:1 read,

> *For the gifts and calling of God are without repentance... I beseech you therefore, brethren, by the mercies of God, that ye PRESENT YOUR BODIES A LIVING SACRIFICE, holy, acceptable unto God, which is your reasonable service.*

Once God calls you, once He gives you that gift, He won't take it back. Therefore, Paul tells us here how to maintain the anointing on a ministry – do something with your body!

The Believer: A Living Sacrifice

God is telling us through the Apostle Paul that we must give our body up as "a living sacrifice."

This is my fortieth year of ministry. When I first got saved, as I mentioned before, I started in the toilet ministry. But that was a ministry, and the time I spent in the ministry of helps wasn't lost time, it was preparation time. I learned a lot serving in the ministry of helps and dealing with people.

For the past thirty years, I've been in a traveling ministry. I have logged over 11 million air miles, and that's just commercially. I don't know how many more I have flown through private air travel with planes I've owned and leased in the past. Some of you know what it's like to travel all the time. At church, you may enjoy a heavy anointing with people being healed, having big crowds, and everything going well. But the next morning when you wake up in your hotel room, you don't even feel saved! You look at yourself in the mirror and say, "Hey, you're the righteousness of God." And your body speaks up, "You sure don't look like it."

That's when you walk by faith. You can't walk by the anointing that's on you in the services. That's when you have to give up your body as a living sacrifice.

Hotel rooms all look alike. They all smell alike. Some of them are just nicer than others, but they're all the same. You get so tired of those four walls! During the day, you pace back and forth, praying, looking at those walls.

Dead Men

I once asked myself, "What am I doing, living in a hotel room? I could be home with my wife and my sons!"

And the Spirit of the Lord rose up in my spirit and said, "Dead men don't gripe!"

You know what happens to a sacrifice? It dies! Dead men

never fight back, either. So, if you're going to make it in the ministry, you can't complain, "So-and-so said this or that about me."

Dead men never get even! Have you ever been in a mortuary and seen a dead man jump out of his coffin, yelling, "You owe me $150?"

You never try to get even with those who come against you in the ministry either. Prophets, like every other Christian, must give up their bodies as a living sacrifice.

Two Requirements for Ministry

Paul continues in Romans 12:2, *"And be not conformed to this world: but be ye transformed by the renewing of your mind, that ye may prove what is that good, and acceptable, and perfect, will of God."*

So, there are two things you've go to do to be in the ministry. First, give your body up as a living sacrifice for what you're called to do, making whatever sacrifice it takes to walk in that calling.

But people don't want to pay that sacrifice. They don't want to pay that preparation time. They don't want to pay that price. They want to jump right into their ministry.

They don't want to carry another man's coat while in the ministry of helps. "Yeah, well maybe I'll do it for a year or two, but not for ten years!", they complain.

See, they don't want to give up their body as a living sacrifice. They want to do what they want to do instead of what God's telling them to do.

Second, renew your mind with the Word of God concerning your calling.

Finding God's Perfect Will

Notice what the Word says will happen when you present

your body as a living sacrifice and renew your mind with the Word of God. When you do something with your body and your mind, then you'll be able to *"…prove what is that good, and acceptable, and perfect, will of God."* That's how you're going to do the perfect will of God in your calling! Many people just do good works in their calling. They never get to the perfect will of God in their calling because they don't do something with their bodies and their minds.

When Jesus appeared to Brother Hagin years ago, He said, "Ninety percent of My ministers don't even get to the first phase of their ministry." Can you imagine that? They don't even get to the first phase! That means, of course, that there are different phases you go through in the ministry.

I want to do the perfect will of God and go through every phase that God has for me in my ministry.

People pray, "Oh Lord, I want to do miracles!" Why do you want to do miracles? Do you want people to look at you and say, "Isn't he a hero?" You're going to have to pay a price if you want to do miracles.

Paul's Recipe for Success

Paul continues in Romans 12:3 saying, *"For I say, through the GRACE GIVEN unto me, to every man that is among you, not to think of himself more highly than he ought to think; but to think soberly, according as GOD HATH DEALT TO EVERY MAN THE MEASURE OF FAITH."*

True, we all have the same measure of ordinary, saving faith. I'm not contradicting that. But in this passage of scripture, Paul's also talking about the measure of faith for ministry. In other words, because our callings are different, it takes more grace and faith to fulfill some of them, even as some require different anointings.

Paul also says, *"…Through the grace given unto me, to every man that is among you, not to think of himself more highly than he ought…"*

Why did Paul mention about grace and staying humble in the same breath? Because one minister has more grace than another minister to get his job done, he's not supposed to think of himself more highly than he thinks of his brother with the smaller ministry. You see, it all originated with God, and not with you! It's done by the grace and the ability He gives, so we can't take the credit for any of it. You may say, "I want a big ministry!" Then you'd better have the grace and the measure of faith necessary to run a big ministry and to believe in the finances!

Do you want to know why many ministers get in trouble financially? Because they launch out into a certain project simply because they want to do it, yet God never gave them the grace or measure of faith to do that kind of work.

Herds of Problems

I've made that mistake. I started a school in my first church in Southern California – grades kindergarten through high school. It caused problem after problem after problem! Parents used to wait outside my office in herds, ready to corner me because of something that happened in the school, or because a teacher had spanked their child!

Finally, I went into the sanctuary and prayed. I said, "God, You are going to have to do something! I'm doing what You told me to do."

He said, "I never told you to start a school! You went to a church growth seminar and they said that every church should have a school. I never gave you the grace or the measure of faith to start a school."

That's why I had so many problems! That's why it was costing so much money! So, the next day, I cancelled the school, and then big herds of parents gathered outside my back door, mad because I was shutting it down.

I learned the hard way that you can't go beyond the grace and faith God has given you for your ministry.

We get in trouble when we add things onto our ministry, saying God told us to do it.

Measures of Pride

A young pastor friend of mine has a huge new building. It seats 5,100 people, and it was filled before it was even completed. Other preachers visit the building and say, "I'm going to do that!" No, God has given that young man the grace and the measure of faith to get that job done.

I was at a ministers' convention once and heard the pastor of a large church get up and say, "God does not bless storefront churches." And I saw 75 percent of those pastors drop their heads in shame. Those young pastors were there to be helped, not destroyed.

That speaker should never have made that statement, because God has given him grace and a measure of faith to accomplish special things. You're not to judge what God has given other people, just because they've got a smaller measure. *"For I say...to every man...not to think of himself more highly than he ought to think...."* Pride will destroy you.

This teaching out of Romans 12 has set many preachers free across this country. They were all thinking, "I'm not having success." I tell them, "Then you're judging success the way the world judges success."

If someone told me, "You're not having success because you built a building that seats 800, and it isn't filled up," I would reply, "I'm just obeying God. I did what God said. He said, 'Put 800 chairs in this building.' I just go day by day. God might say, 'Start a church and give it to someone' – I don't know. I'm just here, obeying God."

Success in the Kingdom

When discouraged, young pastors tell me, "I'm not doing anything for God," I tell them, "Get in your prayer closet and talk to God about that grace and that measure of faith you need. If God gives you grace and a measure of faith for only 50 people, you'll find yourself standing beside those who pastor the world's largest churches in the awards ceremony when you get to heaven. The Lord will tell you the same thing He will tell them. "Well done, thou good and faithful servant."

You see, we get in the flesh and look at success the way the world does. Instead, we must walk in what God has called us to do and look at things from the perspective of the Kingdom of God.

If God tells you to have a television ministry, you need to get in your prayer room to wait before God, and He'll give you the grace and faith to be able to step out and do it. But if God hasn't told you to do that thing that seems so attractive to you, you'd better not do it!

Gifts Differing

Paul confirms all of this in the next verse. *"For as we have many members in one body, and all members have not the same office... Having then gifts differing according to the grace that is given to us, whether prophecy, let us prophesy according to the proportion of faith"* (Romans 12:4, 6). Notice again, that not all members of the Body of Christ hold the same office.

Yet, people today are trying to do what they did in David's time – walk in someone else's grace, or imitate what someone else is doing for God.

David went down to the brook and selected some stones for his slingshot. That was his customary way of fighting, and he had been successful doing it. But King Saul tried to put his own armor, his grace and measure of faith, on David.

David said, "No, it isn't working," so he took off all that

armor and picked up those stones again. They represented the grace and the measure of faith God had given him.

A Lesson for Prophets

Prophets must not try to walk in another prophet's anointing.

Some have said, "Bless God, if that preacher can have an airplane, then I'll get one." No, walk in the grace that God has given to you. The gifts differ according to the grace that is given to us; therefore, the equipment will be different too.

Many preachers take trips to see other ministers' great works. They get inspired and try to imitate them, but you'd better have the same grace and the same measure of faith.

Let's look at Romans 12:6 again. *"Having then gifts differing according to the grace that is given to us...."* The ministry gifts carry different ranks and different anointings. *"...Let us prophesy according to the proportion of faith."*

God never gives a minister a bigger call than his gift of faith. As we saw, this "measure of faith" has nothing to do with personal faith; rather, it is the faith given to enable you to fulfill the work God has called you to do in your rank. No matter what your rank is, you'll be rewarded according to your faithfulness.

Ranking in the Ministry

Ministry ranking is similar to military ranking. The greater your rank within your office, the more people you will affect, either positively or negatively. That's why some people have larger churches than others. They're affecting more people.

When a high-ranking minister is wiped out, all those under him are automatically affected. Therefore, we shouldn't rejoice when one falls and gets hurt, because it will affect all of us in one way or another.

Satan's ranking is paralled with God's ranking, so when one of God's generals knocks out one of Satan's generals, it automatically affects the devils in lower ranks.

The Prophet's Anointing

That's why God gives the prophet a greater measure of faith for ministry. Every true prophet I know has a heavy anointing that was given to him for a reason.

However, in most meetings, people don't even recognize the prophet's anointing when it's present. The prophet's anointing is deeper – it's heavier than other anointings.

I was ministering in a meeting and a heavy anointing came in. The next night, the pastor said, "Well, that was kind of a low-key meeting last night. We need to have it more upbeat."

He missed the whole thing! He didn't realize that there was a prophet's anointing in that auditorium! God was dealing with and ministering to thousands of people in that church. Things were being taken care of in the nation by the Spirit of God.

You don't always have to jump up and down, bang and clang, leap onto the chairs, and everything else. There's a time for all that, but there's also a time when God moves quietly and deeply.

Beyond Your Faith

Paul himself could go no further than his measure of faith. That's where a lot of us get in trouble. We try to go further than what God has called us to do.

For example, if you operate in the gifts, do not feel obligated to perform if the anointing isn't there. If the Spirit doesn't manifest, don't try to force something to happen. If you do, you might open yourself up to a familiar spirit, because you'll be off the Word. If the Spirit isn't leading you to operate in the gifts of the Spirit, but you try to make something happen, then you open yourself up to the enemy to deceive you.

Discerning the Lord's Body

According to Ephesians 4:12, 13, God gave the ministry gifts, *"For the perfecting of the saints, for the work of the ministry, for the edifying of the Body of Christ. Till we all come in the unity of the faith, and of the knowledge of the Son of God, unto a perfect man, unto the measure of the stature of the fullness of Christ."*

All the ministry gifts must recognize each other and the part they play in the Body of Christ for this to be accomplished. They must operate in unity.

The apostle inspires and leads us on to fresh conquests for Christ. The prophet speaks secrets and revelations from the throne of God. The evangelist reminds us of lost souls. The pastor recognizes the need to care for new believers. The teacher studies and teaches the Word of God and the prophet's inspired messages. We must recognize and honor these differences in the offices so that we'll stay in unity.

> *But let a man examine himself, and so let him eat of that bread, and drink of that cup.*
>
> *For he that eateth and drinketh unworthily, eateth and drinketh damnation to himself, not discerning the Lord's body.*
>
> *For this cause many are weak and sickly among you, and many sleep* [die prematurely].
>
> *For if we would judge ourselves, we should not be judged.*
>
> 1 Corinthians 11:28-31

There's a triple meaning here when Paul is talking about "discerning the Lord's Body." First, there's the aspect of discerning what was purchased for us on Calvary: salvation, healing, restoration, and so forth.

The second meaning deals with individual members of the

Body of Christ correctly discerning the other members of the Body; honoring them and the supply they have for the Body of Christ.

The third meaning deals with the Body as a whole discerning the ministry gifts within the Body. Paul is saying that we need to discern the fivefold ministries that God has set into the Body of Christ.

In verse 30, he says the reason why many local churches, as well as individuals, are weak spiritually, and why many die prematurely, is because they do not discern what God has set in the Church. (One reason why the entire Body of Christ is weak today is because it does not discern or hear what the prophets of God are saying to the Body. Prophets speak fresh revelation from God which will cause strength within the Body.)

Discerning the Body of Christ

We also need to discern the different parts of the Body of Christ more clearly. For example, there are different anointings on different churches. Never judge one church against another, because they're all serving a purpose in the Body.

I can think of several examples in one city. One of my friends is a real pastor. He has a tremendous Charismatic church. Another is a teacher who just opens his Bible and flows in that operation and administration. A third has an evangelistic church. Their emphasis is on winning souls.

We're all important to one another. We supply one another. What is tragic is when pastors don't discern the prophet's anointing; especially on a prophet with a proven record. The church needs the prophet's ministry to bring it light.

Pastors have invited me to their churches, saying, "I need some help. Things aren't lining up in the Spirit. Some changes need to be made, and I don't know what to do." Well, a prophet's ministry is one that deals with things in the spirit realm, as God directs him to.

The prophet has the ability (or the grace) to speak into the spirit realm, and set a church back on course spiritually.

For example, a church may be experiencing a real attack against its finances. Under the anointing of the Spirit, a prophet can go into that church, speak into the spirit realm as the Holy Spirit wills, curse that spirit of lack and poverty, and drive it off that ministry. It works the same way with any other kind of satanic attack a church may be experiencing.

I've seen many churches turn completely around and become stronger because a prophet came in and made diverse deposits into that church by the Spirit.

You see, this is a little-known side to a prophet. When a prophet prophesies over a church under the unction of the Holy Spirit, that church can be set on a correct course, and spiritual deposits can be made that will change that church forever.

When the prophet's anointing brings this kind of light, believe the prophet and obey the scriptures.

Now that we are in the new wave, we ministers are going to have to come together and help each other, accurately discerning the different parts in the Body of Christ. The ministry should not be a one-man show.

Discerning the Prophet

There have been times when God has sent me to ministers to speak to them about corrections to make, but they didn't receive it, and some of them died shortly after that. God knew that if corrections weren't made that they wouldn't be around much longer. So, when they rejected the message God told me to give them, they rejected their help.

A man who will not listen to a prophet is not discerning the prophet's ministry, or part, that was set in the Body of Christ. Do you know what will happen to that man? He will become weak spiritually. He will become sickly in his ministry – and he could die prematurely! His ministry or church could also die if he doesn't heed the words that a prophet has said.

Look at that prophet's record. You can go by the man's record, can't you? Suppose a man came to me and said, "Dr. Dufresne, if you will give me $1,000, I will invest it for you, and within 30 days, I'll make you $10,000." If I know the man has 50 years of experience in investments and he's hit it every time, I would listen.

You may not like what the prophet says, but look at his fruit – look at his past record. This is discerning the prophets that God put in the Body of Christ.

Just watch what will happen to pastors who disregard the prophets. All over the land you'll hear people asking, "He has such a big church. What happened? It just dwindled."

"But what happened?"

"The anointing wasn't there anymore."

"But he was such an up-and-coming young man. Oh, he could teach and preach! What happened?"

He didn't listen to what the Spirit of God said through the prophet! He said, "No, I'm not going to obey! This prophet's just old-fashioned, and this is a new day. He's trying to put us in bondage."

The prophet wasn't trying to put him and his church in bondage; he was bringing light on their situation. If the young pastor had listened to the illumination the prophet brought, his church would have prospered. As we saw earlier, that's one reason why God set prophets in the Church.

There have been many times, over the years, that God has

sent me to churches to try to help pastors with different difficulties. The ones that received what God told me, were helped. There are others who didn't receive, and some lost their churches, while others died prematurely.

Discerning the Pastor

God set in the church, first apostles, then prophets, evangelists, pastors, and teachers. All of these ministries are valid. We need to discern every one of them.

God said He set pastors in the Church. That's why I'm so church-oriented. I recognize the pastor's ministry. I don't believe in people running around from church to church, or in holding renegade meetings. Some of you will always be weak in certain areas of your life if you don't discern the office of the pastor and submit to a pastor.

You ministers of the Gospel and traveling ministers, listen to me. Where's your family when you're on the road? You need to discern the pastor's ministry. Your family needs a pastor. They need to be active in a local church, and not just attending. You need a pastor too. I don't care if you do have a ministry. If you're a traveling minister, you need a pastor over your life and family. The pastor isn't to direct your ministry, but your life needs a pastor.

I know preachers whose kids act like a bunch of wild animals. When their dad is off preaching and winning the world, the kids sneak out of the house to "party", and are out riding around on motorcycles on Sunday morning when they should be in church.

First Corinthians 11:31 tells us we need to judge ourselves – the Church needs to judge itself – concerning the spiritual gifts that God has set in the Body of Christ. In other words, we need to discern spiritual things in the Body of Christ

Concerning Spiritual Gifts

Let's look at First Corinthians 12:1, *"Now concerning spiri-*

tual gifts, brethren, I would not have you ignorant."

I've said it in the past, and I've heard other teachers say that this verse should read, *"Now concerning the Holy Ghost...."* But that isn't true. Although Paul is talking about the Holy Ghost to a certain extent here, he's talking more about spiritual things.

Also, that word "gifts" was added by the translators of the King James Version; it actually isn't in the original. This verse should read, *"Now concerning spiritual, brethren, I would not have you stupid or ignorant or misinformed."*

Going down to the fourth verse, it says, *"Now there are diversities of gifts, but the same Spirit."* Notice the word "gifts" is plural. That means the gifts of the Spirit, but it also means the gift ministries that God has set in the Church. God doesn't want us ignorant about the gift ministries — the fivefold offices.

Continuing with verses 5 and 6, *"And there are differences of administrations, but the same Lord. And there are diversities of operations, but it is the same God which worketh all in all."*

"Administrations" means services, ministries, and offices, and Jesus is the Administrator. Jesus wants to be the Administrator of our services. If we allow Him to administrate, the Holy Ghost will be free to manifest Himself. He is the Manifester of what God operates and of what Jesus administrates.

On the other hand, Jesus is the Prophet in the Body of Christ, and He administrates to the prophets, as well as to the other ministries, their services, ministries, and offices.

With that in mind, let's read verse 28, *"And God hath set some in the church, first apostles, secondarily prophets, thirdly teachers, after that miracles, then gifts of healings, helps, governments, diversities of tongues."*

Types of Prophetic Anointings

We saw in First Corinthians 12:6 that there are different operations and different manifestations in a prophet's ministry. Even as there are different types of prophets, they also all have different personalities.

Sometimes they just act differently. You'll be sitting talking to them, and they won't hear a word you say because they're tuned into what God may be saying to them. Or, they'll be standing beside you, and suddenly they'll go off into the Spirit, and God will tell them something about you that will help you.

Also, there are different levels of prophets. You progress in your office and anointing as you mature and grow. Surely God isn't going to put a strong anointing on a man who just got saved. He could have the calling of a prophet, but that doesn't mean he's going to flow under a strong anointing right away. He first must build character, and mature in other ways, just like every other believer.

Jonah was a prophet to the world, but he got self-willed because he didn't want to go to Ninevah. He said, "I'm not going there!" He took off in a ship bound in the opposite direction, and look where he ended up – in the belly of a big fish! That's right, Jonah got vomited up on the beach!

If you try to run from the anointing or the assignment on your life, you'll end up in a disgusting place! I warn you, you'll stink, like Jonah did if you try to run from God!

Actually, you will never be able to run from God once He's called you. You will be miserable doing anything else until the day you die. You will be miserable driving a truck. You will be miserable being a salesman. You'll be miserable in everything you do until you get up and walk in that anointing!

Men and women of God can function in different offices, but they'll be in trouble if they don't concentrate on the primary ministry God has given them.

Naturally, not every gift carries the same anointing, but whatever it is that God sanctified and ordained you to do, you've got to do. You've got to get in that flow and move in it! If you try to do anything else, you'll experience all kinds of problems that could have been avoided if you would have obeyed God.

Settle it right now in your heart, that anything you could want for yourself will never make you as happy or fulfill you as much as walking out God's plan for your life.

The Church's Critical Hours

This is not time for rebellion! What you do now in your ministry is crucial. It's very important right now for everyone in the Body of Christ to be in the right place at the right time. Follow the leading of your spirit. This includes the prophets.

It's critical that the prophets say what the Spirit of God is saying at this time without backing down or worrying about being ridiculed.

What does a prophet do? He speaks for God, and that brings light into the Body of Christ. So, if the prophets are not saying anything, or if they don't have the right people around them, how are they going to speak the things of God, especially when believers don't even discern their gift?

You need to discern what the Spirit of God is saying through the prophets! As we saw earlier, the true prophet of God is a seer. He brings light to the Body of Christ when he prophesies under the unction of the Holy Ghost.

Chapter Four
Glimpses Into the Future

There are many things about the future that I want to share with you. God has been dealing with me about things that will happen in the Church as we enter this last wave of God.

> *And God hath set some in the church, first apostles, secondarily prophets, thirdly teachers, after that miracles, then gifts of healings, helps, governments, diversities of tongues.*
>
> *Are all apostles?....*
>
> 1 Corinthians 12:28, 29

The answer to the last question is, of course not.

Church History Will Repeat Itself

If you'll look at Church history, the Church started out with the twelve apostles of the Lamb laying the original foundation of the Church, so that foundation is complete. Today's apostles, however, build on that foundation, adding their part. Then the prophets, teachers, and other gift ministries add their part.

We saw many evangelists come on the scene at the start of the Healing Revival in 1947. Healings, miracles, signs, and wonders were evident in their meetings.

When the Charismatic Movement swept millions of new

believers into the Church in the 1960's, the Lord raised up pastors to care for them. Twenty years later, they were followed by teachers, who kept things on an even keel.

Now, this era we've been in is about to end. As it ends, it will start all over again with apostles! The Bible says the last shall be first! We're starting to hear a lot about the apostles and the prophets who are coming on the scene.

As we come closer to the time when Jesus returns and the Church Age ends, we're going to see the restoration of the apostle's ministry. They will come to the forefront just as they did at the beginning of the Church Age.

In other words, history is going to repeat itself. The emphasis on the office of the apostle and the prophet to the Body of Christ is one of the things that lies ahead for the Church.

The Prophet's Reward Will Return

He that receiveth you receiveth me, and he that receiveth me receiveth him that sent me.

He that receiveth a prophet in the name of a prophet shall receive a prophet's reward; and he that receiveth a righteous man in the name of a righteous man shall receive a righteous man's reward.

And whosoever shall give to drink unto one of these little ones a cup of cold water only in the name of a disciple, verily I say unto you, he shall in no wise lose his reward.

Matthew 10:40-42

What does a "prophet's reward" mean? The Greek word means, "pay in wages." Spiritually and in the natural, there are rewards.

People say, "I've given to prophets of God. I've given to different ministries, but I haven't gotten any rewards." Well, if you haven't, let's find out why.

On a recent trip, I was ministering in a Sunday morning service, and the Lord said, "This church needs help. I want you to proclaim a reward on these people as they give in the offering this morning for receiving you as a prophet. I want you to proclaim a blessing over them!"

As they came forward, I did what God told me to do. The results were spectacular! By the time the evening service started, people already had wonderful testimonies to give. Their financial reward in higher wages and in other ways started happening to some of them that very day – in addition to the Spirit's reward they had already received.

Elisha's Problem

I went back to the Bible and found some nuggets while reading about the prophets. Let's look first at Second Kings 4. Keep in mind that Elisha is president of this School of the Prophets. One of the prophets in his school died, and his widow came to see Elisha with her problem.

> *Now there cried a certain woman of the wives of the sons of the prophets unto Elisha, saying, Thy servant my husband is dead; and thou knowest that thy servant did fear the Lord: and the creditor is come to take unto him my two sons to be bondmen.*
> 2 Kings 4:1

Notice that the woman's husband feared the Lord.

> *And Elisha said unto her, What shall I do for thee? tell me, what hast thou in the house? And she said, Thine handmaid hath not any thing in the house, save a pot of oil.*
> 2 Kings 4:2

Everyone, no matter how desperate he is, has something that can be multiplied. And those who are not desperately poor have many things they don't use around their house – things that can be used to help finance the next great move of God!

In the coming revival, you're going to start seeing people donate their boats and everything else. Just the stuff we've got laying around our homes can support the ministry! (When I said this in Florida, it didn't go over very well, because they've got big million dollar boats docked outside!)

The Revival Will Be Funded

One afternoon, a friend and I were walking around a marina looking at those boats, and the Lord spoke to me, saying, "All this is laid up for the just."

Wealthy people spend a million dollars for a boat and go out on it two or three times. The owners have to pay large fees to maintain and dock those expensive boats. It's just a waste of money – a rat hole the devil uses to keep money out of the Gospel. Those boats sure would buy a lot of television time!

God said to me, "I'm going to start multiplying with the working of miracles when people start giving to holy men. I want you to proclaim blessings on them when they give to your ministry. Start to teach other ministers to do the same thing so the people can be blessed." (Particularly notice that phrase "holy men.")

Elisha was a holy man. He said to the widow, *"What shall I do for thee. tell me, what hast thou in the house?"* The widow told him she had nothing except a pot of oil. Notice what Elisha said next. *"Go...."*

This story reminds me a little of blind Bartimaeus. He went after his miracle. He made a decision that he was going to get it, it didn't matter what anyone said about him. They told him to shut up, but he kept going after it. He wasn't going to shut up!

We are going to have to start using our faith. We give up too easily. We get discouraged too easily. We need to fight the fight of faith for what belongs to us!

Faith will always go toward the miracle! We see this in John 11 where Jesus kept telling His disciples, "Let's go. Let's go toward the miracle." They were going toward Bethany, where Jesus' friend Lazarus was already in his grave.

Obey the Word of God. Then go toward the miracle, acting like you've already got it. Speak words of faith about your problem, even if the answer hasn't shown up yet. When you pray, believe that you receive. Believe you've got the answer right now. It's already yours, it's settled!

"Well, it doesn't look like it, Dr. Dufresne."

You're going by the natural senses, but I'm going by what the Word says. If the Word says I'm healed, then I'm healed. If the Word says my needs are taken care of, then they're taken care of. I don't care what the devil and all his cohorts (and all their friends in the natural) say. I'm going toward my miracle, glory to God!

Elisha didn't tell the widow what he was going to do to bring about her miracle. All he said was, *"Go, borrow thee vessels abroad of all thy neighbours, even empty vessels; borrow not a few"* (2 Kings 4:3).

Will You Limit the Size of Your Blessing?

That sounds like she's the only one who can limit this blessing! Her miracle will be limited by the number of containers she brings. (I'd get every vessel in town if a prophet told me, "Go get them," because they're going to be filled up!)

Then he told her, *"And when thou art come in, thou shalt shut the door upon thee and upon thy sons, and shalt pour out into all those vessels, and thou shalt set aside that which is full "*(v. 4).

Notice, she obeyed the man of God. *"So she went from him, and shut the door upon her and upon her sons, who brought the vessels to her, and she poured out"* (v. 5). She poured out. You know, you're going to have to obey the Word and give out. Hoarded things aren't going to get you the blessing you want.

"And it came to pass, when the vessels were full, that she said unto her son, Bring me yet a vessel. And he said unto her, There is not a vessel more. And the oil stayed" (v. 6).

That means it stopped flowing. Some people get money, like an inheritance, and they blow it. It runs right through their fingers. It runs out.

Sad to say, most Christians don't know how to handle their money at all. They don't tithe to God, they don't help the poor; they don't do what God says. They try to excuse themselves by saying, "Well, I'm so far in debt, I can't tithe anything."

Start where you're at. Start tithing to God and see what happens. He said in His Word that He changes not. He's the same yesterday, today, and forever!

"Then she came and told the man of God. And he said, Go sell the oil, and pay thy debt, and live thou and thy children of the rest" (v. 7).

How many of you would like to pay your creditors? This widow had so much money left, she lived the rest of her life on it!

Financial Miracles Will Come!

From the things that are in my spirit, I believe we're going to see these same kinds of miracles happen in the future! There's not much time left before the Lord returns. It's going to take a lot of finances to get the job of evangelization done, so we're going to need some working of financial miracles in our lives.

We're going to see some men of God do strange things. One may ask you for your last dime, like Elisha asked the widow. Only this time it won't be a gimmick, as we've seen in the past.

In this fourth chapter of Second Kings, we see Elisha encounter another woman of faith.

"And it fell on a day, that Elisha passed to Shunem, where was a great woman; and she constrained him to eat bread. And so it was, that as oft as he passed by; he turned in thither to eat bread" (v. 8). This was a well-known woman, a wealthy woman who persuaded the prophet to honor her home with his presence.

"I Perceive That This Is An Holy Man"

"And she said unto her husband, Behold now, I perceive that this is an holy man of God, which passeth by us continually" (v. 9). That phrase "holy man" jumped out at me. I said to myself, "I wonder how many people think I'm a holy man?" Have you preachers ever wondered that about yourself?

Too many Christians, including Bible school students, have a bad credit rating. Some live like the world. Some lie like the world. That's why sinners laugh at us. Some don't live godly lives because of the simple fact that they've got the world in them.

The phone rings, and your wife says, "He isn't home right now," and you're sitting right there in the front room. Before you know it, you've seared your conscience to the point that you don't tell the truth anymore, and you don't even realize that you're no longer a holy man of God. You're a sinner!

While I was in Florida, God told me, "The reason why a lot of people aren't getting returns and being blessed is because they're not giving to holy men."

This great woman in Shunem perceived that Elisha was a holy man, and she asked her husband, *"Let us make a little chamber, I pray thee, on the wall; and let us set for him there a bed, a table, and a stool, and a candlestick: and it shall be when he cometh to us, that he shall turn in thither"* (v. 10).

Some teach that this prophet's chamber was actually in the front of the house, over the porch. They believe it was a larger beautiful room and furnished nice. In fact, they think the "stool" was really a throne built especially for the prophet.

"We've got a prophet's quarters," pastors have boasted to me. I've stayed in those prophet's quarters. They're furnished with used furniture dating from 1942. The bed is rickety and everything else is beat up, too.

Faithfulness Will Be Rewarded

Now we're coming to the part with the nuggets.

> *And it fell on a day, that he* [Elisha] *came thither, and he turned into the chamber, and lay there.*
>
> *And he said to Gehazi his servant, Call this Shunammite. And when he had called her, she stood before him.*
>
> *And he said unto him, Say now unto her, Behold, thou hast been CAREFUL for us with all this CARE; what is to be done for thee? wouldest thou be spoken for to the king, or to the captain of the host? And she answered, I dwell among mine own people.*
> 2 Kings 4:11-13

Those words "careful" and "care" jumped off the page when I was meditating on that passage one day. Elisha was saying, "You were very careful to take care of us."

God told me we have not been very careful to take care of the men of God in our day.

When you don't take care of the men of God, you're not taking care of Jesus.

You've got to realize that the fivefold ministry is a gift from Jesus, the Head of the Church. So, we must be careful to take care of the men of God.

Some churches that haven't done this properly are deep in debt, even to the point of just paying the interest on their loans.

You see, when spiritual leaders are not treated right by churches or their ministries, it will always take a toll on them and their ministry.

"What Do You Need?"

The return on her giving came to the woman of Shunem when Elisha asked her, "...*What is to be done for thee?...*" Oh, I like that! I'd never done that until God told me, "When people bless you and take care of you, I want you to start asking them, 'Pastor, what do you need in this church? Do you need a new addition to your building?'"

You'd be surprised how many pastors fight me about paying my airfare when they invite me to come preach in their church! They want me to pay for everything, and then take all of their meeting expenses out of my love offering. That isn't being careful to take care of the man of God.

You know, if you can't take care of a man of God, don't invite him. I'm tired of all this jiving. "Oh, brother, we love you, but...." I'm just telling you why people aren't getting blessed! Ministers are going to have to start being honest in their dealings with others.

When I want to hold a special meeting in our church, like our Fresh Oil Conference, I count the cost first and then I start putting money aside. That way we can take care of our speakers properly. We won't ever dip into their love offering to pay bills.

The reason many believers haven't been getting blessed is because they haven't been giving to holy men of God. They've been giving because people put emotional pressure on them through the mail or other gimmicks.

Prophets Will Get Results

The woman who honored the prophet is about to get her reward. It was suggested to her, "...*wouldest thou be spoken*

for to the king, or to the captain of the host? And she answered the
servant, I dwell among mine own people." She meant, that she
already had social status. She was a wealthy woman because
it took a lot of money to build that addition onto her house for
the prophet.

> *And he said, What then is to be done for her? And*
> *Gehazi answered, Verily she hath no child, and her*
> *husband is old.*
>
> *And he said, Call her. And when he had called*
> *her, she stood in the door.*
>
> *And he said, About this season, according to the*
> *time of life, thou shalt embrace a son. And she said,*
> *Nay, my lord, thou man of God, do not lie unto thine*
> *handmaid.* (II Kings 4:14-16)

The Miracle Came!

"About this season, according to the time of life, thou shalt
embrace a son... And the woman conceived, and bare a son at the
season that Elisha had said unto her, according to the time of life."
God performed a miracle for this barren couple.

Fifteen to eighteen years passed between this verse and
then next, for the story that is building in this chapter leaps
ahead to when the boy is grown.

> *And when the child was grown, it fell on a day,*
> *that he went out to his father to the reapers. And he*
> *said unto his father, My head, my head. And he said*
> *to a lad, Carry him to his mother. And when he had*
> *taken him, and brought him to his mother, he sat on*
> *her knees till noon, and then died.*
> (2 Kings 4:18-20)

It looked like the devil stole her miracle. The boy died. It
looked like the prophet of God missed it.

In the good times, we gain a lot of knowledge out of the

Word of God. But when bad things happen, stay hooked up to the Word.

For example, if you start having financial problems, you'll be tempted to say, "Well, tithing doesn't work," and if you're not careful, you'll stop tithing.

The Word is always true. Just stay with it, and that situation in your life will change. The Word will never change, so the situation has to. The Word is the same yesterday, today, and forever. That's the way we ought to be in our walk with God.

Fight for Your Miracle!

If a man of God gives you a prophecy, and if he's a holy man of God, then stand on that word. Those blessings are going to come on you. But you're going to have to fight the fight of faith for them because the enemy wants to steal that word, that prophecy, from you. He will try to steal your health, too. Resist the devil, don't fight people; fight the fight of faith for what belongs to you.

Healing belongs to you! Prosperity belongs to you! It's God's will for you! So don't listen to people that would talk you out of faith.

We don't get in the Word of God and fight for what belongs to us! We need to get in line with the Word of God and do what it says! Fight the good fight of faith!

A Test of Great Faith

The woman's son died. *"And she went up, and laid him on the bed of the man of God, and shut the door upon him, and went out"* (v. 21).

I want you to look at this woman's faith. She knew about the prophet's ministry.

In those days, people went to the prophet of God for guidance. Actually, the prophet of God gave the people God's Word for their lives because that was the only way they could get guidance from God. Today, we have the Holy Spirit within us, giving us guidance. We don't go to the prophet or any other minister for guidance. Yet, God will use them to confirm what He has already said to us. But why not have the same kind of faith this great woman had? If we did, we'd get the results she got!

She knew about the anointing that was on the prophet's mantle! She placed her dead son's body on the prophet's bed, walked out and shut the door.

> *And she called unto her husband, and said, Send me, I pray thee, one of the young men, and one of the asses, that I may run to the man of God, and come again. And he said, Wherefore wilt thou go to him today? it is neither new moon, nor Sabbath. And she said, It shall be well.*
>
> 2 Kings 4:22, 23

Her husband said, "Why are you going to see the prophet?"

And she said, "It will be all right."

She didn't even tell him their son was dead!

Concentrating on the Results

Faith people who believe in the end results don't blab about all the problems they're having. This woman knew what the end results were going to be. I like this woman's faith. She had the God-kind of faith, not the flaky-kind of faith!

She reminds me of the woman with the issue of blood who said, "If I may but touch his garment, I shall be healed." She also reminds me of blind Bartimaeus. He locked into faith and got his miracle, too.

How many of you want results in your life? You can't ride the fence.

We're going to have to believe what the Word of God says. We're going to have to get back to the Bible for our finances, healing, and every other area of life, walking holy before God.

Better Returns on Your Giving

"Then she saddled an ass, and said to her servant, Drive, and go forward; slack not thy riding from me, except I bid thee" (vs. 24).

She got into her Cadillac. Not everyone was wealthy enough to own a donkey in those days. She and the servant moved! This woman was in a hurry.

> *So she went and came unto the man of God to mount Carmel. And it came to pass, when the man of God saw her afar off, that he said to Gehazi his servant, Behold, yonder is that Shunammite: Run now, I pray thee, to meet her, and say unto her, is it well with thee? is it well with thy husband? is it well with the child? And she answered, It is well.*
> (2 Kings 4:25, 26)

She didn't talk about her problem. She said, "It is well." Quit talking about your problems. You can deal with them with faith.

You can't say, "Well, that problem really isn't there." No, that's getting into Christian Science. We don't deny reality; we deal with it. How do we deal with it? With the Word of God!

> *And when she came to the man of God to the hill, she caught him by the feet: but Gehazi came near to thrust her away. And the man of God said, Let her alone; for her soul is vexed within her: and the Lord hath hid it from me, and hath not told me.*
> (2 Kings 4:27)

She didn't mess around! She caught the prophet by the feet. Gehazi tried to push her away. Notice that the prophet didn't know about her problem. Prophets don't know everything. Elisha said, "It's hidden from me. I don't know what her problem is."

Then she said, *"Did I desire a son of my lord? Did I not say, Do not deceive me?"* (v. 28).

I like the faith of this woman. Most people would have quit then.

The Importance of Standing in Faith

She said, "You're a prophet of God. And I got my pay in wages. But that pay didn't last. My child died. Now, don't you deceive me. Don't you lie to me!"

> *Then he said to Gehazi, Gird up thy loins, and take my staff in thine hand and go thy way: if thou meet any man, salute him not; and if any salute thee, answer him not again: and lay my staff upon the face of the child.*

(2 Kings 4:29)

Sometimes a staff member isn't good enough.

"And the mother of the child said, As the Lord liveth, and as thy soul liveth, I will not leave thee...."

There's something about making up your mind to stand in faith that makes God move on your behalf. Brother Smith Wigglesworth said, "You make the decision that you're going to stand in faith, and God will go over a million people just to get to you." God honors faith!

And Elisha followed her.

> *And Gehazi passed on before them, and laid the staff upon the face of the child; but there was neither voice, nor hearing. Wherefore he went again to meet him, and told him, saying, The child is not awaked.*

> *And when Elisha was come into the house, behold, the child was dead, and laid upon his bed.*
>
> *He went in therefore, and shut the door upon them twain, and prayed unto the Lord.*
>
> (2 Kings 4:31-33)

No Fast-Food Prayer Life

A lot of believers give up because they don't get instant results. Don't get in a hurry.

I want you to see that the man of God went into that room to get results. He prayed.

Study the mininstries of Jesus, John Alexander Dowie, Maria Woodworth-Etter, Smith Wigglesworth, John G. Lake, and others. They dealt with people differently, as the Spirit led them. Jesus spit on people. Sometimes He'd make mud and put it in their eyes.

But our generation is in a hurry. We enter a sick room and expect instant results. Just because we eat at fast-food restaurants doesn't mean we can do that with our prayer life.

There are times when you're going to have to get before God and pray for a season, even though it would be easier to lay your flesh down on the couch and turn the television set on, saying, "Well, in the Name of Jesus, I believe that I receive it. Amen."

> *And he went up, and lay upon the child, and put his mouth upon his mouth, and his eyes upon his eyes, and his hands upon his hands: and he stretched himself upon the child; and the flesh of the child waxed warm.*
>
> *Then he returned, and walked in the house to and fro; and went up, and stretched himself upon him: and the child sneezed seven times, and the child opened his eyes.*   (2 Kings 4:34, 35)

I want you to know that this woman got her prophet's pay in wages right then, about eighteen years later.

Claim Your Prophet's Reward

God told me that there will be a time when people are going to need a miracle, and if you have taken care of a man of God, you've got a prophet's reward coming. You can stand in faith and get it. You have a right to it. I know there have been lots of gimmicks used to squeeze money out of believers, but this isn't a gimmick. This is the Word of God.

The woman got her return. She got her pay in wages. She got her child raised from the dead! Years after taking care of a prophet, her prophet's reward still worked.

Praise God, we're going to see the prophet's ministry come on the scene. It doesn't do away with the other gift ministries; it adds to them.

Some of you need your finances raised from the dead. Some of you need your bodies raised from the death bed. God has provided a way for each one of us to get our needs met.

The Coming Wave of Healing

One of the things God has told me about the future concerns a mighty wave of healing. He said, "We are entering the day when there is going to be such a revival of healing that hospitals are going to be emptied out by the power of God." The Lord told me in 1999, when I had a vision of heaven, that 2006 would be a year of marvels, and then He told me that this last end-time revival will be up and running by 2007.

He continued, "People are going to come to churches where that healing power is flowing. People are going to be set free. It's going to hurt the medical profession so much, that lawsuits will start coming against the Church from that industry." (They'll claim we are practicing medicine without a license.) I am not against doctors! Praise God for doctors.

Praise God for hospitals. They are not the ones who heal, but God will use doctors to help people. What I'm saying is that Jesus is the Healer!

I'm getting in position for this revival. I'm ready for the next wave. It's coming! It's starting to happen now – a little bit here and a little bit there. It's going to get stronger and stronger.

It is vital that all of us be in the right position, and you'll be able to flow with it.

That's why we wrote the book *Fresh Oil From Heaven* – to get this message out into the Body of Christ so people will get into position.

Prosper Through the Prophet's Anointing

Are you listening to me, Church? What is the Spirit of God saying through the prophets? Listen to what they are saying, and you'll have insight into what is about to happen.

When the prophets say good times are coming in the economy, it's the time to buy and sell. But when they say, "Don't get into debt," pull back, and you will make it through that period. The prophet's anointing brings light, and when you obey, you'll propser!

There are more prophets around than you think. They're all over this land. In fact, there are prophets who are placed over cities and nations. That's why we need to pray for the prophets to come forth. And they are! The prophets are coming!

The gift ministries' job is to equip the saints, so if you don't know what you're supposed to do in the Body of Christ, let the pastor, the evangelist, the teacher, the prophet, and the apostle help instruct and equip you.

Obedience always creates an atmosphere for miracles! We saw that with the Shunammite woman. Young prophets need to listen to this advice. Don't try to figure everything out in your head. Just obey the voice of the Lord!

The Prophet's Helpers

I don't know why, but the devil hates prophets! He will try to destroy their family. He will try to destroy a prophet any way he can. That's why it's important for a prophet to have the right people around him.

When you have been around a prophet's ministry, you learn what it takes to pull on the prophet's mantle.

So, it's important that prophets have people around them who understand the prophet's ministry, and who can help the prophet yield to his anointing.

The Sunammite woman was a help to the prophet. She supplied a place for him, but she also knew how to make a demand on his mantle, and receive from him.

Chapter Five
A New Era

I want to share out of my heart where we are in time. What time is it? You know, God will reveal to the prophets what He is going to do on this earth before He does it. What is about to happen in the Body of Christ? Would you like to know? Some of you may know if the Lord has been speaking to you, but we are in a new era.

I was at a church where we were having a week-long Fresh Oil Conference. It was our own meeting, and the pastor was letting us use his church building. It was the week of Dad Hagin's memorial service, so we flew down to Tulsa to be in the service.

When I was at the memorial service, the Lord spoke to me and said, "An era has come to an end and a new era has begun."

We are in a new era right now, and this is what I want to explain to you.

There are several things I see lacking in the Body of Christ and among ministers. For one thing, young ministers don't recognize greatness in men or in the Body of Christ. I didn't say great men – I said greatness *in* men.

I remember when Dad Sumrall was alive, and I had asked a pastor, "When was the last time you had Dad Sumrall in?"

"Well, Brother Ed, we had him in once, but then he got talking about his *Feed the Hungry* program, so I didn't have him back anymore."

I told that pastor, "You didn't know who you had in your pulpit. You had Dr. Sumrall, yes; but you had Smith Wigglesworth, you had Howard Carter, you had all those men through the years that he was around and had imparted to him."

See, that's the lacking thing; the body of Christ doesn't recognize greatness that can be passed down from generation to generation. Think about it!

I was around Dad Sumrall for fifteen years. He told me that he adopted me as one of his sons. We would go on trips together, and he would sit me up in first class with him on the airplanes to teach and mentor me. What an honor! It was worth every dime – whatever I paid to be around that kind of anointing!

You know, some pastors gripe about paying the jet fuel to bring a minister to their church, but do you put a value on money or do you put a value on being around the anointing? I paid whatever it cost to get Dad Sumrall to my church, and it paid off. I received mighty impartations from him. If you're more worried about money and being money-minded, you'll miss out on an impartation.

Smith Wigglesworth's Prophecy

In 1939 World War II was about ready to break out. Dr. Lester Sumrall was in his twenties. He was working in a Bible school in England and he got to know Smith Wigglesworth. He read his books and heard about his ministry. He had been going over and visiting Smith Wigglesworth in his home for several years. Every other week he would visit him. Smith Wigglesworth would also have Brother Sumrall to speak at his conventions.

One day, Lester Sumrall went to tell Smith Wigglesworth that a police officer had come to his door and told him that everyone who was not an English citizen would have to leave the country. Hitler was threatening to come across the English Channel, so all foreigners had to leave.

The young Sumrall explained to the elder minister, "I came to say goodbye to you. I appreciate all that you have put into me." Now, here was a young minister in his twenties, and here is a man in his eighties. The man in his twenties wants it, and the man in his eighties, wanted to give it to somebody.

Smith Wigglesworth told the young minister, "I want to bless you." So he held him and said, "Lord, everything that I have, bless him with it! Give it to him!" Smith Wigglesworth started weeping as he pulled Brother Sumrall in closer.

"He was a big man, and as he held me close into him, his tears rolled off his face and they would hit me on my forehead and run down my face," Brother Sumrall explained.

Wigglesworth cried saying, "I probably won't see you again now. My job is almost finished."

As he continued to pray, he cried out, "I see it, I see it!"

Brother Sumrall asked, "What do you see? What do you see?"

He said, "I see a healing revival coming right after World War II. It'll be so easy to get people healed. I see it! I see it! I won't be here for it, but you will be." And there was a healing revival right after the war.

He continued to prophesy, "I see another one. I see people of all different denominations being filled with the Holy Ghost." That was the Charismatic Revival. God raised up people during that era, like the Full Gospel Businessmen.

Then Brother Wigglesworth continued, "I see another move of God. I see auditoriums full of people, coming with notebooks. There will be a wave of teaching on faith and healing." We did experience that wave he saw, and we called it the Word of Faith movement.

Then he prophesied, "After that, after the third wave," he started sobbing, "I see the last-days revival that's going to usher in the precious fruit of the earth. It will be the greatest revival this world has ever seen! It's going to be a wave of the gifts of the Spirit. The ministry gifts will be flowing on this planet Earth. I see hospitals being emptied out, and they will bring the sick to the churches where they allow the Holy Ghost to move."

The Last Days Prophecy

When I was at Brother Hagin's funeral, God said to me, "An era has come to an end and a new era has begun." What is that new era? That last-days revival that Smith Wigglesworth prophesied about!

God told me, "That prophecy Smith Wigglesworth gave is for your day, get that in your mouth! You tell the people, as a prophet of God, to get that prophecy in their mouth and they'll start having revival wherever they go."

God told me how He had prepared Brother Hagin during the Healing Revival and the Charismatic Revival to lead the body of Christ in the Word of Faith movement. Although Brother Hagin had ministered for years, his ministry didn't really take off until his era came. When his era came, his ministry reached all over the world through radio, books and tapes. Why? Because that was his era!

But that era came to an end when Dad Hagin went home to be with the Lord. Now we are in a new era. That doesn't mean God is doing away with the teaching of faith, but many of the Word of Faith people will not go with this new era. They'll live in the past era, and they'll dry up and become another denomination.

When one era ends and another begins, we must be ready to move with God. There is nothing like the deadness of an era that has come to an end, and people still trying to live in that past era. That's why there are dead churches. They held onto that old era and they didn't move forward with God.

That's one of the problems today; people don't know how to move with the Holy Ghost. Are you listening to me? Those in the healing wave fought those in the charismatic wave. They didn't go with the next era, or the teaching wave.

I don't know about you, but I'm going with the Holy Ghost! Miracles are coming! An outpouring of the gifts of the Spirit is coming! The very beginnings of the greatest revival this earth has ever seen is moving and I want to be right in the middle of it!

Mentors in the Faith

God will put you with men who will mentor you. God put Lester Sumrall with Smith Wigglesworth who imparted into his life.

Dr. Sumrall was a mentor to me. One night Dad Sumrall called me to his hotel room and said, "Come here, Brother Ed. Watch this! I am going to sign this $5 million deal on this television station and I don't have any money in the bank, but God told me to buy it!" And he just signed his name to it. Even though he didn't have the money to buy it at the time he signed that contract. Every dollar for it came in by the time the money was due.

Dr. Sumrall got that spirit of faith from Smith Wigglesworth. Some things have to be caught, they can't be taught!

As a young man, Lester Sumrall would travel any length of time to get to Smith Wigglesworth's house, but people today are too busy to be around the man of God. They're too busy to be around the anointing.

There are some pastors and ministers who will drop everything and come to my meetings. They'll come at their own expense. They'll do anything to be around this anoint-

73

ing; and they'll receive impartations.

A Vision in the Throne Room

On October 7, 1999, I was in a meeting in Oakland, California. It was just one of those meetings you'd like to be able to just push a button and have it repeat every place you go. It was a barn-burner! People were laying all over the floor under the power of God.

After the meeting, the pastor was leading me out of the auditorium to the elevator that led to another floor of their four-story building. They pushed the elevator button, and when the door opened up, I felt my spirit leaving my body. I said, "Lord, I don't know if I can go that far," and when I said that, I left my body. My body fell to the ground and my oldest son grabbed my head.

I found myself in Heaven, face down. I could see sandals and part of a beautiful blue robe. I believe that it was Jesus, since He's the Head of the Church. He began speaking to me about the last-days revival, and my part in it. He said, "This is your era. It's the time I've been training you for."

He talked to me about California and about an earthquake that would happen there. He talked to me about many different things that were about to happen.

He said, "Now, you must tell the people. You've got to tell them that judgment is coming to the Church." He didn't tell me when that would happen, but Dad Hagin got caught up in the Spirit during the 2003 Winter Bible Seminar and prophesied about the years 2004 through 2006. He prophesied that 2004 would be a year for more. Then he said that 2005 would be a year of judgment. Every arena of our lives will be judged. That means that judgment is coming to the Church, but if we judge ourselves, we won't be judged.

When I was in Heaven, God told me that in 2007 this new revival will be up and running. He also told me that 2006 will be a year of marvels. We're going to just marvel at what God does. But before that, we must judge ourselves to see if we are living in obedience to God's Word in every arena of our lives. Judge yourself to see if you are walking in love. Judge yourself in the way you are treating your spouse. You've got to judge yourself on your attitude about money.

Ministers must judge themselves. There will be some ministers that won't be here at the end of 2005. There are some ministers on the forefront that won't be here anymore. We must all judge ourselves in every arena of life.

The Bible says in First Corinthians 12 that if we would judge ourselves, then we won't be judged. So, that's easy – judge yourself with the Word of God and you won't be judged.

I've already made up my mind that I am going to make it through 2005.

If you'll pray in the Holy Ghost, He will show you what needs to be changed. If there's a wrong attitude toward anyone in your family, get rid of it. What about any wrong attitudes towards your pastor? What about wrong attitudes toward giving tithes and offerings? Get rid of stinginess. Judge yourself.

Cancer-killing Endowment

As I was in Heaven, I felt a hand touch me on my head, and Jesus told me that He was giving me an endowment to kill cancer, and that I would begin seeing the healing endowment He placed in my right hand in 1971 increase until, eventually, 100 percent of those I minister to who have cancer will be healed.

He also told me that the fivefold offices will be operating at their full potential in these last days. He then spent time telling me about the pastoral office more than the other offices, and He said this last-days revival is going to be in the local church.

The Door to the Supernatural

Jesus appeared to Dad Hagin and told him, "Ninety percent of My ministers never get into the first phase of the ministry I have for them, and that's why many of them die prematurely."

If you are not walking in the will of God, then you are walking in disobedience, and if you are walking in disobedience, the devil has an open door to attack you. If someone is not in God's will, then they can't claim God's best, which is healing; so that's the reason many of them die prematurely.

In a lot of places I minister, many people come forward who have had accidents, but Christians shouldn't be having accidents tripping, falling down all the time, getting beat up! Even under the Old Testament, if they just stayed in obedience to the covenant, they were protected from having accidents. Even as the Israelites wandered in the desert for forty years, after having been delivered from Egypt, the Bible tells us that their clothes didn't even wear out; and we have a better covenant!

If you walk in love, there is no devil in hell that can touch you. You won't be falling, or be in a wreck; you won't have people stealing money from you because you are protected. Psalm 103:4 tells us that we are redeemed from destruction. Anything that would harm or destroy, we are redeemed from! But one step out of love, and you become vulnerable.

Now, if you get in unforgiveness, or get a fighting spirit toward people, then you get onto the devil's territory. Christians miss it by not walking in love.

Another place believers miss it is by not taking time to pray in the Holy Ghost. Why do you think God blessed you with the baptism of the Holy Ghost? One reason is so you could pray in tongues, which is the door to the supernatural.

We can know things before they happen if we'll be sensitive to the Spirit of God. I know things in my spirit, not because of the office I stand in, but because I take time to pray in other tongues. There is a door to the supernatural that we can all enter in by praying in the Holy Ghost. Yet, praying in the Spirit is one of the lacking things in the Body of Christ.

If people were sensitive to the Spirit of God, (which is done through praying in tongues), they would not be having accidents. If they were praying in the Holy Ghost, the Spirit of God would tell them not to go that way. There are many hardships that could be avoided if people would just learn to follow the Spirit of God.

Speaking in Other Tongues

Another thing lacking in the Body of Christ is discernment. Many don't discern spiritual things, and I believe I know why. In some recent services, I asked the people, "How many of you pray in the Spirit at least thirty minutes every day? Now don't lie to the Holy Ghost. Don't raise your hand if you are not doing it. How many pray thirty minutes or more?" Only four or five people raised their hands. Then out of my spirit I heard myself say, "That's why you live more in the natural than you do in the supernatural."

Praying in the Holy Ghost is what opens the door to the gifts of the Spirit, and the gifts of the Spirit are weapons. Praying in the Holy Ghost will expose any works of the devil. Every pastor ought to have the gifts of the Spirit operating in his ministry; he will need them in pastoring a church. These are lacking things in many churches today.

God wants you to live more in the supernatural. If you are living in the supernatural, you'll know who to run around with, what to buy and what not to buy; and you wouldn't be having the pastor pray for you all the time because you are always in trouble.

Tongues is the door to the supernatural. That's where we

are supposed to live. Those who live life in the natural instead of the Spirit are getting all beat up; but supernatural people should be excelling. Some people are working 24/7, trying to make ends meet. I'll guarantee you that if you'd pray in the Holy Ghost at least half an hour a day, God would give you ideas and you wouldn't have to work such long hours. You'd be able to bring your family to church and all these other things would fall into place.

Praying in the Holy Ghost is the door to the supernatural. You see, when you get into the door of the supernatural, you'll know things; you will have the spirit of knowing. Because Christians have the Holy Spirit inside, it's possible to live here on this earth and never make a mistake – it's possible! Not everybody does, because we are human, but it's possible. If we would pray in the Holy Ghost, it's possible that we would never lose any money in any investment that we invest in, if we would follow the leading of the Holy Spirit – it's possible. But we do things we regret because we don't take time to pray and get it clear in our spirits what steps we should take.

In the meeting where I asked those to raise their hands who prayed in the Holy Ghost at least thirty minutes a day, there were several rows of pastors and ministers who didn't raise their hands. No wonder the Lord had said to me earlier, "In most pulpits, most preaching is mental preaching and not spirit preaching." So what do they have? A mental church. That's why they have psychology and everything else in the church – because it's mental preaching.

Another one of the lacking things is learning the patterns of God. God has patterns in a man's ministry. I know there are four phases in my ministry.

Now I am in my fourth phase. I just went from my third phase, and now I am in my fourth phase of the prophet's mantle. Plus, since I'm going to nations, I've stepped up into another office. But I am in the beginning part of the fourth phase of my ministry. Every minister should know these things about his ministry! They should know what phase they are in if they are spending time talking with God. If you pray in the Holy Ghost, He'll let you know.

Progressing in the Anointing

As a young Christian I learned how to believe God when He told me to quit my job so that I could be the foreman on the new church we were building. I didn't get paid for it, but I learned how to believe God for money to support my family and to pay my rent. That's how I developed my faith.

You'll never get anywhere in the work of God unless you prove yourself faithful by getting involved in your local church, and allow yourself to be developed and be mentored. He was developing me while I was serving in that local church.

If you want to be developed, you need to get hooked up to your spiritual supply. What is your spiritual supply? That's where God sends you to be fed and developed spiritually–that's your supply!

Someone may say, "Well, they offended me and I'm leaving!"

You had better be careful about that if God told you to be there, because by leaving, you will be leaving your supply.

The problem with many Christians is that they go to the church that has the best nursery instead of going where God told them to go. If you do go somewhere other than where God's called you, you'll never be mentored there; you'll not fulfill all God has for you unless you get to the place where your supply is, and be faithful there.

I got saved in a Full Gospel church. But in 1971 things were changing and the faith message was coming to prominence in the Body of Christ. That era was about ready to start. The Lord was getting ready to put me into that camp because that was where my supply was.

While I was the foreman on the construction of our new church building, someone handed me a pamphlet that read, *World Convention of the Full Gospel Businessmen*. As I looked at it, the Lord said, "I want you there."

I said, "Lord, right now I don't have the money to go to that meeting."

He said, "Sell your house!"

Now don't go selling your house unless God tells you to, but God told me to sell my house, and that was the best investment I ever made! I was investing into the future of my ministry!

At the time He told me that, I was in the ministry of helps. The ministry of helps is a dignified ministry. It isn't in the same category as the fivefold offices, but it is a ministry. Really, the ministry of helps is where you start out in ministry. Then, if the call of God is on you to stand in a fivefold office, you'll start being promoted from there. But if you can't be faithful in the ministry of helps, promotion won't come, no matter what you're called to.

I've seen those in the ministry of helps that God was getting ready to promote, and they got into offense and left their spiritual supply, and it put them ten years behind in their ministry – all because they got into offense and they didn't realize that they were doing it.

If you'll spend time praying in the Holy Ghost, it will help you stay free from offense. You know, you can tell when a person doesn't pray in the Holy Ghost, because they are crabby all the time. They are moody, not pliable, and not workable.

Here I was as a young Christian, serving in the ministry of helps in my local church and finishing up the construction of our new building. What if in the middle of that construction job I had gotten into offense and took off, leaving my local church and my supply? I'd never be where I am at today. If I had never worked in the ministry of helps, I wouldn't be in the ministry I am in now because the ministry of helps is where you start if you are to be promoted to the fivefold ministry.

If you believe you are called to the fivefold ministry, get involved in the ministry of helps.

You may say, "Well, I don't know what I am called to do." Then start out in your natural abilities and you will end up in your supernatural abilities. If you are a carpenter, do carpenter work. If you are good at cleaning, then clean in the local church. Do whatever you can do.

I was serving in the ministry of helps when the Lord said to me, "Go to that Full Gospel Businessmen's Convention," so I put my house up for sale, and it sold in three days. I set my family up in an apartment and took off to go to those meetings.

I had no idea that this was so ordained of God, for it was at that convention that I was introduced to three ministers that I had never heard of – Kenneth Hagin, John Osteen and Kenneth Copeland. I heard all three of them minister in a youth group meeting of about 1,200 people down in a hotel basement.

When John Osteen ministered, God said to me, "There's going to be a day when you are going to pastor for awhile."

I said, "No, I'm not going to pastor. I want to be in the ministry of helps, that's my deal. I am not a preacher! I'm not going to get up in front of people. I don't even like people." Back then I didn't like people, much less want to get up in front of them. But God developed me and I got my mind renewed with the Word of God, and later I did pastor for eight years. I started with twelve people and it grew from there.

I remember before I started pastoring, I told God, "Well, I've got to have a sign that I'm to pastor." A businessman went and rented a building and bought fifty chairs, and came to me and said, "You're supposed to pastor here." There weren't any people there – only empty chairs.

But after we started services, for a whole week there was a white dove that came and stood under that church door all day long; and God said to me, "That's your sign!" I was just a young pastor, and I didn't know any better than to ask God for a sign; but God met me where I was at and gave me that sign. Of course, I know better than to ask for signs today, for we are to be led by the Spirit of God and not by signs.

As I sat in the Convention Center listening to John Osteen minister, God said, "I want you to follow John Osteen and pattern your church after his." After I started my first church, I used to go to his pastors meetings, and I was blessed by his ministry. He taught us about pastoring a church by the Holy Ghost, and something got inside of me.

Later, as Brother Copeland got up to speak at that Full Gospel Businessmen's Convention, God said, "Follow him as one of your teachers in the area of the covenant," and I've done that.

When Brother Hagin ministered, God again spoke to me and said, "Follow Brother Hagin the closest, he's to be your spiritual father." And I did follow him closely until he went home to be with the Lord.

Now see, God hooked us up. That wasn't done by man. God put that together.

God put me with all those men. God put me with my supply.

Then Dad Sumrall came into my life in 1979. At that time I had pastored for eight years and had over a thousand people coming to that church.

In 1979 I was reading the book *Run with the Vision*, by Dr. Lester Sumrall, and I just broke down and wept. I read it all the way through till 3:00 am, just crying and weeping. God said, "I am going to put this apostle in your life." I laughed like Sarah did when she got the news that God said she would have a baby.

God said, "He's another one of your supplies and I want you to follow him." I laughed to think that I could be associated closely with such a man, but the Lord rebuked me for it, and two weeks later I got a phone call.

My secretary came running into my office saying, "Dr. Sumrall is on the line."

I said, "Quit kidding me!"

"No, it's him!" she insisted.

I said, "Ah, come on now!

"No, it's really him!"

So I went along with it and answered the phone. "Hello?"

"Is this Pastor Dufresne?" I could've recognized that voice anywhere.

"Yes, this is he," I answered stunned.

"Norvel Hayes told me I should come to your church. When can I come?"

Then it dawned on me – this is him! This is the man who went all over the world! This is the man who cast the devil out of that girl that was bitten by the devils!

And now I was shaking, "How about in two weeks?"

"I'll be there. Goodbye!" and that was it.

That's how Dr. Sumrall came into my life and we hit it off. He loved me and I loved Him. I was with him for fifteen years.

Now listen, all those men that God told me to follow closely don't live here anymore; they've all gone home, except for Brother Copeland. God told me the other day, "You are to be commended for staying with those I told you to follow. Most of My ministers get into offense and leave those I told them to be with."

But I stayed right with them! I followed Brother Hagin the closest because God told me that I'd have a ministry similar to his.

God said to me, "You are to be commended for doing what I told you to do, and you got something from each one of those men. They passed something to you, they imparted something." So, when I'm ministering, you don't get just Ed Dufresne anymore. You get Smith Wigglesworth, Howard Carter, Dad Hagin, Dad Sumrall – that's the plan of God.

There's a lot of teaching on spiritual fathers today, but you can't be fathered by someone unless God connected you with them.

Be around those that God connects you with. Be around those who stand in the same office you are called to. If you are called to be a pastor, you need to be connected to a pastor.

Footprints to Follow

But now we are in a new era. Now I am in my era. This is the era that I have been training for and looking toward for the past thirty-nine years. This is my era. I'm a changed man. Something has happened to me because I'm coming into to what I have been trained for.

People under training are tempted to be anxious or unsettled. That's why we must run our race with patience. It takes patience during those seasons of training before you will walk into the fullness of God's plan for your life.

When I came into this new era, God spoke to me while I was in Abakan, Russia, "Now you are going to the nations!" And the nations have opened up.

We are in a new era!

Last New Year's Eve, while getting ready to preach in Anaheim, California, I said, "Lord, who's going to train me now?

The men You told me to follow are all gone."

I stood in that service on New Year's Eve talking to the Lord, and tears were running down my face. "Lord, now I am going into a new year and my dad, Brother Hagin, is gone. Who do you want me to follow now?"

He spoke to me. "Do you remember when you first got saved thirty-nine years ago in that Full Gospel church?"

"Yes Sir," I answered.

He continued, "They took you in the back room to pray with you for you to receive the baptism of the Holy Ghost. Do you remember the picture they had on the wall?"

"Yes, it was a picture of a beach that had footprints in the sand that were made by Jesus."

God spoke, "Now that Jesus has left the earth, it's the ministry gifts, those who walk in the fivefold offices that are making footprints for others to follow. Paul said, *'Be ye followers of me, even as I also am of Christ,'* and he made footprints after Jesus left, and they followed him."

I said, "Yes, those men I was to follow are all gone; they are not making footprints anymore."

"Now it's time for you to make footprints for this next generation to follow," He instructed.

I said, "Lord, that's an awesome responsibility!"

"I'll help you," He said. "You go! You have come into your time now!"

For a complete list of tapes
and books by Dr. Ed Dufresne,
and to be on his mailing list,
please write:

Ed Dufresne Ministries
P.O. Box 1010
Murrieta, CA 92564

(951) 696-9258

www.eddufresne.org